598   15489

Birdwatching
on estuaries, coast and sea

Clare Lloyd

**With drawings by
Norman Arlott**

SEVERN
HOUSE

SEVERN HOUSE NATURALIST'S LIBRARY

To my father

British Library Cataloguing in Publication Data
Lloyd, Clare
Birdwatching on estuaries, coast and sea.
 (The Severn House Naturalist's Library).
 1. Sea birds – Europe
 1. Title
 598.2'94   QL690.A1
 ISBN 0-7278-2003-6

Published by Severn House Publishers Limited
144–146 New Bond Street
London W1Y 9FD

Text © Clare Lloyd 1981
Drawings © Severn House Publishers Limited 1981

Editorial Ian Jackson
Design Michael Stannard

Filmset by Tameside Filmsetting Limited, Ashton-under-Lyne, Lancashire

Printed and bound by Hazell Watson and Viney Ltd,
Aylesbury, Buckinghamshire

Contents

1 **The coastal habitats**   **6**
  What the birds need   13
2 **How the birds cope**   **25**
3 **Introducing the birds**   **46**
  Naming birds   47
  The coastal species   49
4 **What you will see**   **70**
  Some basic advice   70
  The birds on a sandy beach 75; in sand dunes
  80; on mudflats 86; on a saltmarsh 92; on a
  shingle beach 95; on a rocky shore 96;
  on cliffs and islands 99; out at sea 108;
  on urban waterfronts 110
5 **What else you can do**   **113**
  Records and field notes   113
  Photographing birds   114
  Reserves   117
  Seawatching   119
  Surveys and censuses   122
  Oiled, sick and injured birds   127
  Ringing and bird observatories   129
  Other studies   136
6 **Conservation of coastal birds**   **137**
Appendices
  I Scientific names of birds mentioned in text   152
  II Useful addresses   153
Further reading   **155**
Acknowledgements   **157**
Index   **158**

1 The coastal habitats

Nowhere in Britain is more than 112 kilometres from the sea, and this is also true of neighbouring countries apart from France. The coastline, stretching southwestwards from the arctic expanses of northern Scandinavia to the subtropics of west Africa, is folded into a series of bays and promontories, fjords and islands which offer birds many suitable places in which to live. At least 110 different species, from seabirds and ducks to waders and birds of prey, regularly use the coast for feeding and breeding.

Nearly all the places where birds occur on the coast of northwest Europe are easily accessible to birdwatchers. In fact many of the largest cities are situated near the coast, often on estuaries; for example, London, Southampton, Liverpool, Edinburgh, Dublin, Belfast, Rotterdam, Antwerp and Bordeaux. Human activity on the coast tends to be centred around sandy beaches and the artificial waterfronts of built-up areas. Much of the coast elsewhere may seem desolate and uninteresting by comparison. The endless carpet of mud and sand stretching away to the skyline in an estuary at low tide appears lifeless at first glance, without any possible use to Man, suitable only for reclamation from the sea and development into a holiday resort or commercial dock. The people who believe this fail to appreciate the abundance of life the mud supports and how the estuary's intricate structure makes it an important habitat for all kinds of wildlife. Birds congregate on the coast in enormous numbers at certain times of year. There can be few more spectacular sights than a wader roost at high tide or a seabird colony at the peak of the nesting season.

Birds are easy to see on the coast but what makes the coasts of Britain and the rest of northwest Europe so special? Why are the birds there and what are they doing? Finally, how can the muddy wastes of an estuary be so vital to birds?

To answer some of these questions, we must examine the different coastal habitats in which birds live. For birds the coastline is divided broadly into beaches, estuaries and urban waterfronts. Within each of these there are several different habitats and the seven basic coastal ones are: sandy beaches, sand dunes, shingle beaches, rocky shores and cliffs, mudflats, saltmarsh and the sea itself. Estuaries include all of these habitats but saltmarsh is particularly typical of estuarine areas and rarely found anywhere else. Urban waterfronts contain mudflats, shingle and sometimes even sand banks, as well as waste ground near the sea which can be

Figure 1 A flock of at least 1,500 Knot in a high tide roost. The incoming water has covered the feeding grounds and the birds have gathered on an exposed spit to rest and preen. In the background are two much larger Oystercatchers.

used by birds. Apart from saltmarsh, all the different habitats also occur elsewhere on the coastline. Each habitat or combination of them provides for the birds' two basic needs which are food and, when necessary, a safe place in which to nest. The structure of each habitat and the factors which control its formation determine both the abundance and diversity of all the animals present. These are linked together with external factors, such as temperature and salinity, in a delicately balanced web known as an ecosystem.

The coast is constantly changing on both long-term and short-term time scales. The long-term changes have been, and still are being caused by the patterns of change in world climate. During the Pleistocene Era, which started about one million years ago, four successive Ice Ages wrapped the earth's north and south poles and the regions around them in permanent ice. Water was locked in the ice caps and the level of the sea fell (see figure 2). When ice cover was at its maximum, the sea was as much as 150 metres below today's level. Between the Ice Ages came interglacial periods when most of the ice caps melted, causing a rise in sea levels. With ice cover at its minimum, sea levels were up to 150 metres above where they are today. For about the last 5,000 years sea levels have remained constant and the coastline has changed little. We are currently in the fourth interglacial period and the land masses are still readjusting after their release from the last glaciation's load of ice. This produces a gradual movement in an island like Britain, where Scotland is rising and England is sinking, both at about two millimetres a year, which also affects the shape of the coast.

In addition to their effect on sea levels the Ice Ages played an important part in the formation of coastal habitats for birds. Lengths of coast were

7

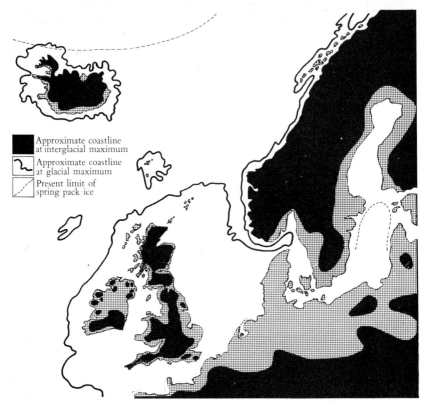

Approximate coastline
at interglacial maximum

Approximate coastline
at glacial maximum

Present limit of
spring pack ice

Figure 2 The coastline of Europe changed during the Pleistocene Ice Ages as the sea levels rose and fell. At the height of the glaciations, water locked in ice sheets caused a lowering of sea levels and land bridges joined Britain, Ireland, Scandinavia, and much of northwest Europe. During inter-glacial periods, when the ice sheets melted, the sea rose and drowned the continental shelf leaving only a few islands exposed.

exposed by the falling sea and scraped by ice sheets, then submerged again when sea levels rose. Drowned valleys produced shallow inlets or estuaries at river mouths, for example the Tamar, Dee and Forth in Britain and the Shannon, Elbe, Rhine and Garonne elsewhere in Europe. Fjords formed where the sea flooded steep-sided glacial valleys. The ice wore away soft rock faster than hard, leaving projecting headlands, off-shore stacks and islands. This is how the typically indented coastline of northwest Europe was formed. The glaciations also affected the salinity and depth of coastal seas, and subsequent cyclic changes in world climate

Figure 3 The Dunlin, like most waders, has a distinctive breeding and non-breeding plumage. The body feathers are moulted twice a year; in spring they are replaced by the bright chestnut mantle, streaked breast and black belly (above), and in autumn the new feathers give the bird a greyish back and white underparts.

8

have controlled their temperature and fauna.

Estuaries are especially important to birds because they offer a particularly wide range of different habitats (see figure 5), and almost all contain extensive areas of intertidal mudflats, saltmarsh or rocky shore. The intertidal zone lies between the average high and low water levels and is very rich in the invertebrate life which forms the diet of many kinds of birds. An estuary changes comparatively rapidly as material is removed (erosion) and supplied (deposition) by currents and tides. The tide flows in twice a day from the sea and the river or lake feeding the estuary supplies a steady flow of fresh water. Fresh water is lighter than salt water and flows out over the tidal influx causing strong currents and thorough mixing. Estuarine plants and animals must be able to stand salt water; several species of invertebrate found in estuaries are simply the salt-tolerant forms of freshwater species which have moved into estuaries to avoid competition. Existing estuaries are geologically very young; all have been formed since the last Ice Age, and so many of the species found in them are at a relatively primitive stage of evolution.

The currents, amount of wave action, salinity levels and oxygen content of estuarine waters determine which invertebrates can live there, and this in turn affects the bird population. Estuary waters are often sheltered by headlands or rocky shores at their mouth which protect muddy or sandy habitats inside. The material which is deposited from the water to create these estuarine habitats comes either from rivers or from the sea. The majority of estuaries in Britain and elsewhere in northern Europe receive most material from the sea. The heaviest deposits settle out first near the estuary mouth in the form of gravel banks. Next the sand and finally the silt (forming mud) gather at the edges of the estuary where the water flows slowly. The reverse is true of estuaries such as those of the Rhône and Loire in France, where the rivers deposit material as sand in the upper reaches, and silt near the sea; deltas are formed in this way at the estuary mouth.

Urban waterfronts also provide a number of changing habitats for birds (see figure 6), although these are usually more suitable for feeding than nesting. Reclamation of land from the sea and industrial development involve constant artificial change which is often to the birds' advantage. The first stage is usually to build a sea wall or dyke across an estuary mouth or out from an existing sea wall. The intertidal area enclosed forms a lagoon which dries out gradually into a marsh with pools, and later into land dry enough for agriculture or urban development. Many birds find rich feeding during the early drying out stages, and when the area is later ploughed or bulldozed and then left fallow, birds are able to use it for feeding and resting. Urban waterfronts are also

Figure 4 The Common Sandpiper and Snipe are waders common on the coast; both breed mainly inland and visit the coast in autumn and winter. Common Sandpipers (above) have a trilling call and typical bobbing action on landing. When flushed from cover, Snipe use a characteristic swerving flight known as jinking.

Figure 5 The main habitats in an estuary with the sand and mudflats exposed at low tide. The variety of places to live makes an estuary particularly attractive to birds and an interesting site for birdwatchers.

used by gulls and terns for roosting, as well as for feeding. Gulls and, occasionally, Oystercatchers nest on buildings in seaside towns, and similar behaviour has been reported in Little Terns from the eastern United States. In central Dublin Common Terns nested first on a disused coal dump and later on reclamation pans near the docks proving how even naturally timid birds can become accustomed to Man.

Short-term changes also occur in the habitats themselves. Rocky shores are broken up by the eroding force of the sea into boulders and stones, then to pebbles and finally to sand and mud. These in turn are moved about by the tide or wind so that, in common with the large-scale changes in the whole estuary, each habitat is perpetually changing. Sometimes changes follow a sequence. A beach elongates into a spit and the mudflat which forms in the shelter of its lea shore changes gradually into a saltmarsh, and eventually into a grassy meadow. This is one example of the natural succession of habitats which takes place on the coast all the

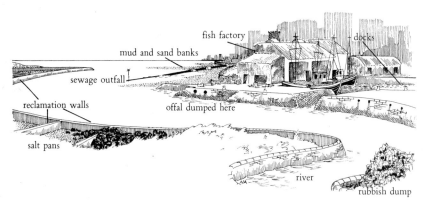

Figure 6 The habitats on an urban waterfront support a wide variety of birds, such as gulls, terns and Oystercatchers.

time, and is critical in determining whether or not an area is suitable for birds.

Finally, there are several other reasons why the coasts of Britain and northwest Europe are especially important for birds. The comparatively warm winters on these coasts attract birds from inland and much further north during the winter months. Many travel westwards to winter on estuaries and other parts of the British and Irish coastlines. The exceptionally rich feeding in estuaries supports migrant birds when they stop off to moult, or to replenish fat supplies needed to fuel their long-distance flight between northern nesting grounds and winter quarters even further south. The prevailing southwesterly winds and currents on the coast of northwest Europe (see figure 7) cause erosion and deposition and the

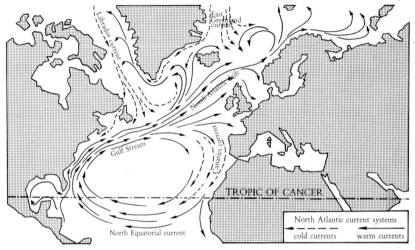

Figure 7 The coasts of Britain, Ireland and Norway are positioned at the junction of warm currents flowing northwards from the central Atlantic and southerly flowing currents bearing cold water from the Arctic. The mixing of these currents causes turbulence and upwelling of nutrients from the deep water layers, and conditions are ideal for abundant marine life including fish, whales and seabirds.

natural succession of habitats, which in turn provides a variety of places where birds can live. Lastly, fishing grounds in shallow waters over the continental shelves where oceanic currents mingle give the seabirds a rich food supply.

What the birds need

Different birds have different requirements for food and nest sites. A wader such as a Ringed Plover feeds on invertebrates and needs an open sandy beach on which to nest; it lives mostly on estuaries or beaches. A Guillemot, on the other hand, is found ashore only on sheer cliffs, often those of offshore islands. It requires a rocky ledge on which to breed and a food supply of fish from the sea nearby. Structural changes on the coast are matched by corresponding sequences of local bird species. Certain kinds of waders prefer to feed on mudflats, others are more typical of saltmarsh, and a few waders but plenty of landbirds occur in the meadow which is the final stage in this particular succession.

All birds obtain their food through a precisely balanced network of supply and demand known, in ecological terms, as a food chain. Every habitat has its own arrangement of food chains (see figure 8). Food chains are an important part of all ecosystems but here we need only consider those in typical coastal habitats such as mudflats and the open sea. These are comparable to the more familiar food chains on land.

The basic process upon which all food chains depend is the harnessing of energy from the sun to fuel growth in the lowest organisms, known as the primary producers. In a terrestrial food chain such as that in figure 8, the primary producers are plants. These use oxygen and sunlight to manufacture carbohydrates by the process of photosynthesis. This requires chlorophyll which is found in the plants' green parts, especially their leaves. Some carbohydrates are broken down during respiration to produce energy for growth. Primary producers provide food and, via the process of respiration, energy for the primary consumers or herbivores of the food chain, for example, cows. These are able to grow and reproduce and in turn provide a source of energy for the secondary consumers, the carnivores, which may themselves be the food of animals in the next stage of the food chain, and so on. In our terrestrial system, cows are eaten by Man. Each stage or trophic level of the food chain is in balance with the preceding and following ones, and natural wastes produced eventually decay and re-enter the system as nutrients for primary production. The size of organisms usually increases from the bottom to the top of the food chain and the numbers typically form a pyramid. For example, a cow eats millions of blades of grass in its lifetime but Man eats only a

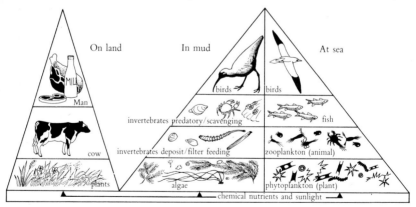

Figure 8 Simplified food chains for inland and coastal habitats. In each, the top predators are relatively scarce compared with the abundance of life lower down the chain, so that numbers or biomass typically form a pyramid.

few cows in his. The top position in the chain is often occupied by a predator such as Man or, in coastal habitats, birds. Different levels of the food chain are usually interlinked so that a food web, rather than a simple chain, exists.

The primary producers in a muddy estuary are minute plant-like organisms called algae, particularly diatoms, which live in the interstitial spaces between grains of mud, and use light, oxygen and nutrients for growth and reproduction. The next stage is less straightforward than in the equivalent terrestrial food chain because relatively few algae are eaten directly by the primary consumers. The herbivorous invertebrates living in mud feed mainly on detritus or organic material which is suspended in the water around them and settles out onto the surface of the mud. Deposit-feeding invertebrates, such as the bivalve mollusc *Tellina* (see figure 9), siphon food including algae from the mud's surface, whilst filter-feeding animals like the lugworm (also illustrated) sieve their food from a stream of water drawn through the burrow or, in molluscs,

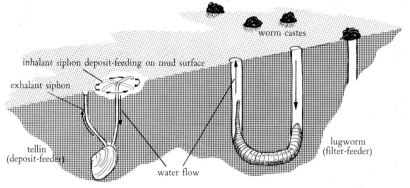

Figure 9 Invertebrates living in the mud obtain their food by filter- or deposit-feeding. The lugworm draws water through its burrow and filters out food particles without ever having to visit the surface. Many deposit-feeders like the tellin also remain buried but extend a siphon to 'hoover up' food particles from the surface. These are brought down into the animal's shell cavity in a current of water.

through the shell cavity. Carnivorous invertebrates, the secondary consumers of this particular food chain, include crustaceans such as crabs and shrimps, and echinoderms like starfish. Other predators are fish – plaice, flounders and dabs. Grey mullet also live in estuaries but they usually short-circuit the food chain by feeding as herbivores, grazing blue-green algae from the mud's surface. Birds are the most abundant and important predators in estuaries, and they take fish and a variety of invertebrates, including those already mentioned and illustrated, from all trophic levels. Most of the birds associated with estuary food chains are waders, but diving ducks, Shags, grebes and divers also sometimes feed on mud banks when they are submerged by the tide.

The food chain in the open sea is similar to that of the mudflat. The primary producers, instead of being wedged into interstitial spaces, are tiny plant-like organisms known collectively as phytoplankton which float freely in the sea in vast numbers. These require light as energy from the sun and nutrients, often supplied from deep water by upwelling currents, for growth and reproduction. Phytoplankton are the food of small animals, the zooplankton, floating in the sea. These are also present in enormous numbers, and include both primary and secondary consumers as some species prey on others. Many species of invertebrates which live their adult life in the intertidal zone and also certain fish have specially adapted planktonic larvae. Some seabirds, mainly petrels such as the Fulmar, act as secondary consumers and feed directly on zooplankton. Some kinds of zooplankton are abundant in surface waters only by night, and others only by day, and so they perform daily vertical migrations in the sea (see figure 10). This can affect the feeding rhythms of seabirds preying on them, and may explain why some seabirds, especially in the tropics and southern hemisphere, forage mainly at night. Most zooplankton are consumed by fish and these in turn by larger fish. Seabirds are important top predators in the food chain and most of them eat fish. Shoaling fish, particularly sprats, sandeels and herrings off northwest Europe, are often selected as food species because they are the easiest to catch in large numbers. Sometimes the birds rely on predators, like mackerel or tuna fish and porpoises in the tropics, to drive shoals of small fish into surface waters where they can catch them.

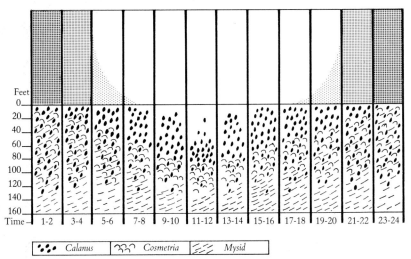

Figure 10 Many marine zooplankton make daily vertical migrations to the surface and this influences the fish and seabirds feeding on them. Here three crustaceans are all abundant at the sea surface at night. *Cosmetria* performs a migration *en masse* and few remain deep down at night. *Mysid* extends its vertical range upwards through the other species to the surface. *Calanus* is absent from the surface only around midday. (After Russell and Yonge.)

The coast also offers a large range of suitable nesting places for birds. The main needs of a breeding bird are a safe place to nest free from disturbance and predators, especially ground ones, and a reliable food supply within its foraging range. This varies from a few hundred metres to thousands of kilometres, depending on the species of bird. Nest sites in coastal habitats are described in detail below; they include beach tidelines, shingle spits, lagoons and saltpans, dune slacks, saltings, offshore islands and stacks, cliffs and even buildings.

Birdwatching may begin simply as the identification of the different species seen, but it becomes increasingly interesting if one can appreciate how the birds fit into the general pattern of their environment. Each bird is part of a community which includes birds of the same species and many others, and this exists in every habitat. As the coast is changing all the time, the bird communities come and go according to the types of habitat available. This becomes clear if each coastal habitat is considered in turn, with the factors which affect it, and the bird community each supports.

Sandy beaches

Erosion and deposition both take place on a sandy beach. Waves breaking on a steeply sloping beach tend to scoop material back into the sea, whilst material is deposited by waves on a horizontal beach or sheltered shore where currents are slow enough to allow particles to settle out of the water. Waves almost always approach a beach, whether of sand or shingle, at an angle, rather than parallel to it, but the water runs off at right-angles to the line of the beach (see figure 11). As a result, solid material carried obliquely up the beach by the waves is brought straight down by the backwash, and ends up several metres further along the shoreline than before. This long-shore drift, as it is known, can gradually move huge amounts of shingle or sand along the length of the beach, and

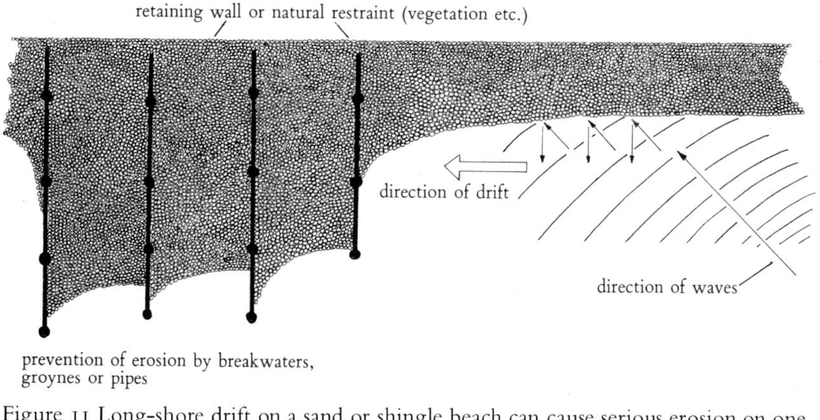

retaining wall or natural restraint (vegetation etc.)

direction of drift

direction of waves

prevention of erosion by breakwaters, groynes or pipes

Figure 11 Long-shore drift on a sand or shingle beach can cause serious erosion on one part of the shore and elsewhere the growth of huge spits (see figure 14).

cause serious erosion which is sometimes reduced artificially by building groynes or breakwaters. At Holderness, Humberside the coast has retreated by one to six metres a year for the last ten centuries. Storm damage speeds up the process; the beaches at Covehithe, Suffolk were eroded by nearly eleven metres in only two hours during exceptional storms on New Year's Eve in 1952. There have been attempts to prevent the sea's erosion by building sea walls around parts of the English coast and other low lying countries bordering the North Sea. Sand dunes which develop naturally from sandy beaches are sometimes stabilised artificially by planting marram grass and conifers as protection against the sea.

The most interesting parts of the beach for birds are the intertidal zone, the water's edge and the tideline left by the most recent high tide, as well as the one furthest up the beach left by the spring tides. Invertebrates buried in the intertidal sands form the main food for waders at low tide, but their distribution and local abundance depends on how much wave action the beach receives or, in an estuary, on how saline the water is. Algae, particularly diatoms, need light for photosynthesis and if the sand is regularly disturbed, these and other invertebrates are easily swept away although diatoms can lie dormant if buried temporarily. Invertebrate life on sheltered beaches is especially rich. The interstitial fauna thrives, and debris settles out from the comparatively slow-moving water to provide food for deposit-feeders like burrowing worms, and for filter-feeders like cockles and mussels. Carnivorous and scavenging invertebrates such as the burrowing starfish, brittle stars and various crustaceans like crabs and shrimps also live on sheltered sandy beaches. All these species are the prey of waders which forage by walking into shallow water to catch the animals out of their burrows or by probing into the sand at low tide.

Occasionally invertebrates are washed up the beach as the tide advances or caught unawares out of their burrows as the tide recedes. These are food for waders, typically Sanderlings, which feed by running up and down the water's edge. The tideline at the top of the beach supplies enough enriching nutrients from the decay of weed, flotsam and other rubbish left there, to encourage the growth of salt-resistant plants such as orache and sandworts. These in turn shelter scavenging invertebrates, especially burrowing sandhoppers, which are ideal food for waders like Turnstones and Ringed Plovers, and insects which attract Skylarks, Shore Larks and pipits.

Sand dunes

The coast tends to be very windy as the land heats faster than the sea by day causing air to rise and produce an onshore breeze. At night the sea cools more slowly than the land and breezes blow offshore. The wind blows the sand into a system of dunes rather in the way that waves erode and deposit sand or shingle on beaches. A wind of only sixteen kilometres an hour is sufficient to move sand and so dunes form easily where there are large expanses of sand to feed them, whether inland as in the Brecklands of East Anglia and in the Sahara Desert or on the coast. To begin with, embryo dunes are formed by the wind and these are gradually invaded by vegetation, especially couch grass, which is resistant to being constantly buried by sand. The vegetation stabilises the dune and forms a barrier to the wind so that there is erosion on the windward side and accretion on the landward side which results in the dune moving inland at a rate of up to seven metres a year. This mobile dune becomes a static dune only when it leaves the strong wind zone on the beach, by which time more embryo dunes have formed to seaward. In this way a series of parallel dunes is built up, and all stages of development are present simultaneously with the oldest ones furthest inland.

Dunes are a relatively poor habitat for birds although they are interesting botanically. The vegetation provides insects and seeds for larks and finches, and the small mammal population, mainly mice and shrews, attracts birds of prey such as Kestrels, Short-eared Owls and occasionally harriers. The flat-bottomed valleys between dunes are called dune slacks, and are usually sheltered from the wind. Slacks are often sites for gull or tern nesting colonies and their pools are used by wildfowl in winter.

Figure 12 Mature sand dunes at Studland, Dorset, stabilised by marram grass and heather. In the distance, the last stages in the succession of habitats is marked by buckthorn scrub. Pipits, Skylarks and finches and a few Kestrels are the most typical birds to be found in dunes.

Marram grass is sometimes deliberately planted to stabilise the dunes and this speeds up the natural succession to buckthorn and birch scrub. These are terrestrial habitats outside the scope of this book but they are also rich in birdlife.

In western Scotland, especially in the Outer Hebridean islands, and in isolated parts of western Ireland, a peculiar habitat known as machair exists on the flat coastal plains behind dune systems. Machair is a type of particularly rich grassland which grows on shell sand blown over the bedrock. It is greatly valued by local farmers for grazing animals and saving hay, and the calcium enriched soil also grows fine crops. Machair is an exceptionally good feeding and nesting habitat for waders, mainly Dunlin, Ringed Plovers, Oystercatchers and Lapwings. An estimated twelve to sixteen per cent of all Ringed Plovers and four to nine per cent of Dunlin breeding in Britain nest in machair in the Outer Hebrides. Unfortunately modern land use is threatening to make this rare habitat unsuitable for birds.

Mudflats

When silt settles out of water on the most sheltered shores, often in estuaries, a gradual succession from sandy mud to intertidal mudflats and saltmarsh takes place. Mucous produced by algae living in the interstitial spaces in the mud cements the silt and prevents erosion by the tide. As the substrate of mud grows thicker, plants become established from floating seeds. These will germinate only if they are exposed from the water for a certain length of time, usually at least fifty hours; this ensures that they start to grow only on substrate not regularly covered by high tides. The first plants to colonise the mud are especially resistant to saltwater. They slow down or eventually prevent water circulation and more silt accumulates so that the level of the mudflat rises steadily. A mudflat with plants on it can grow at the rate of up to twenty centimetres a year, but without plants the level increases by less than two millimetres. As the mud rises, it is covered by sea water for less and less time by each series of high tides, and plants and animals with a lower toleration of salt become established on the mud bank.

The richest invertebrate fauna and birdlife are found on areas of coast with mixtures of mud and sand, often in estuaries. Soft mud without sand is less productive because the mud does not allow the circulation of water and oxygen essential for life. Only certain bacteria can survive in such conditions and these extract oxygen from sulphates in the mud leaving behind sulphides which colour the mud black. Very muddy estuaries and those polluted by untreated sewage or chemical effluent (both of which also deprive invertebrates of oxygen) are characterised by a black surface below which, where even bacteria cannot live, the mud retains its normal colour.

Rotting vegetation and other detritus in the mud and sand provides food for a large number of burrowing worms as any bait-collector will confirm. Filter-feeders including molluscs, fan worms and burrowing shrimps which live in the mud also form the diet of birds foraging on the mudflats. Waders probe the mud with their long bills and extract invertebrates whilst ducks dabble in shallow pools left by the tide. The exact ways in which birds find and collect their food are described in the next chapter. Weed growing on the mud, particularly eel grass and sea lettuce, is grazed by Brent Geese and Shelducks. Most mudflats are almost completely covered by every high tide so that they provide no nesting sites for birds, but because feeding is so rich, especially where mud is mixed

Figure 13 Sand and mudflats on the Wash, East Anglia, an area which holds on average 175,500 waders and 24,500 wildfowl in winter. The casts are typical of lugworms which live in open-ended burrows and are the favourite food of long-billed waders.

with sand, mudflats support masses of waders and wildfowl on migration or during the winter. The birds feed on the mud when the tides permit and gather into vast flocks in isolated places to roost at high water.

Saltmarshes

Saltmarsh is the temperate equivalent of mangrove swamp found in tropical regions. Mangrove swamp and coral reef are the only coastal habitats in the world not found in northern Europe. Saltmarshes develop on the higher levels of mud- or sandflats, above the average high tide level for neap tides. Water drains into and from the marshes through a system of muddy creeks and pools which are the home of marine invertebrates tolerant of regular immersion in sea water. The highest part of the marsh, at its inland edge, is grassy and often used for grazing cattle. This is the last stage in the succession, rarely flooded by the sea, and colonised by entirely terrestrial, though salt-resistant plants and animals. The saltmarsh itself represents the transitional zone between land and sea, and the distribution of the different kinds of plants and invertebrates reflects the salinity and amount of immersion by the tide that each part of the marsh receives.

Three separate types of saltmarsh are found in northwest Europe. In eastern Ireland, west and northwest Britain, Scandinavia and Schleswig-Holstein in north Germany, marshes are mainly of sand and grass. Salt-marshes in southwest Scotland, eastern England, Holland, Belgium and the rest of northern Germany contain less grass and mainly silt. Those in southwest Ireland grow on peat. Around the southern North Sea salt-marshes have been artificially stabilised to prevent erosion and to speed up their development into meadow by planting the cord grass Spartina.

One species of this plant introduced accidentally to England from North America was found to have cross-bred with the local cord grass in Southampton Water. This in turn produced a vigorously fertile hybrid, first noted there in 1870, which has since been planted deliberately to stabilise saltmarshes around the English Channel and North Sea, and even exported to Australia and New Zealand. The hybrid is so hardy and persistent that before long it also spread naturally to many other estuaries in Britain and Ireland. Its swift growth, however, threatens to clog saltmarshes and drainage channels and this is now causing serious problems in many places.

Saltmarshes provide birds with both food and shelter for nesting. Invertebrates in the channels and pools and muddy marsh edges are also typical of the mudflats; these parts of the marsh are favourite feeding places for waders, ducks and sometimes Brent Geese. Numerous insects and seeds in the vegetated areas of marsh attract pipits, larks, finches, wagtails, Teal and Mallard. Redshanks, Dunlin, Black-headed Gulls and sometimes terns are the usual species found breeding on saltmarsh, although their nests are often threatened by flooding on spring high tides.

Figure 14 The shingle spit at Hurst Castle, Hampshire and Keyhaven saltmarsh on the inland (left) side are good habitats for waders and terns. Note the distinct curve in the shoreline, typical of shingle spits.

Shingle beaches

Long-shore drift also affects shingle beaches, causing erosion and the formation of long spits. The Orfordness spit in Suffolk has been growing at over twelve metres a year since the twelfth century. Shingle spits like this are relatively permanent structures, but younger spits are often broken up by winter gales. When vegetated, spits are favoured nesting places for gulls and terns as they offer nest cover and safety from most ground predators. Nearly half of all the Roseate Terns breeding in north-west Europe once nested on shingle islands off Wexford, southeast Ireland until these were destroyed by the sea between 1975 and 1977, leaving the birds with no alternative nesting site.

Shingle beaches have rather poor invertebrate fauna because of the abrasion produced by constant wave action. A few animals, notably lugworms, manage to live under the pebbles and provide a source of food for birds, particularly Turnstones and Oystercatchers. Invertebrates and birds, again mainly waders, are more numerous on the sheltered inland side of shingle spits where a shallow inlet, lagoon or eventually a salt-marsh forms. The tideline on a shingle beach provides some food for waders, and also nesting cover for terns, Ringed Plovers and Oyster-catchers.

Rocky shores and cliffs

Rocky shores are the commonest of all coastal habitats in northwest Europe, but are largely absent from the southern coasts of the North Sea. Their fauna is the most diverse of any of the habitats considered here. The

Figure 15 A rocky shore in Guernsey rising to cliffs and constantly lashed by waves. Purple Sandpipers, Turnstones and Oystercatchers find food in the rock pools at low tide, and diving species like auks and Shags feed on the shoals of fish which come close inshore on calm days.

exact number of different animals present depends mainly on the exposure of the shore to wave action and to weather, particularly low winter temperatures. Diversity is greatest on the warmer south and west coasts, and where the warm Gulf Stream washes western Ireland, south-west Britain and northwest France.

Birds feed mainly in the intertidal zone although diving duck and sea-birds such as Shags forage at high tide. A rocky shore is usually subject to high levels of wave action, especially if it is steep or situated on an exposed coastline. Most animals live in crevices in the rock or are firmly attached to it so that the birds feeding on them, such as the Purple Sandpiper,

Turnstone and Oystercatcher, must use special techniques. Where rock rises into boulder scree or cliffs, colonial seabirds often breed in large numbers. Some nest on open ledges on the cliff and others in crevices or amongst boulders at the foot of the cliff, whilst more burrow into grassy slopes. These birds feed out at sea or just offshore.

Open sea

Coastal seas of northwest Europe lie over a broad continental shelf and are characteristically shallow and especially productive because of the mixing of oceanic currents offshore, and local upwelling caused by water running off the land in rivers (see figure 16). The productivity of the world's oceans, in terms of the richness of bird and fish life and all other levels of the food chain, is determined mainly by the availability of light and nutrients for the growth of phytoplankton. The oceanic currents, like the wind belts in the atmosphere above, encircle the globe in opposite directions. Where conflicting currents touch (convergences), they mix and cause upwelling of vital nutrients from the depths of the ocean, with a rich flush of phytoplankton and other forms of life. In the tropics currents are poorly defined so that upwelling is minimal except near land and seabirds adapt their foraging behaviour to the collection of sparsely

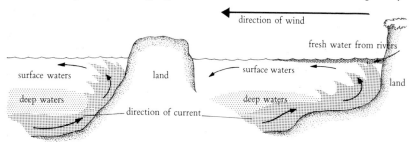

Figure 16 Upwelling currents bring essential mineral nutrients to the surface from deep water and cause rich productivity at all stages in the food chain. Upwelling occurs at sea where surface currents meet or in the lea of offshore islands. In tropical oceans, where productivity is otherwise low, shoaling fish and seabirds are concentrated around archipelagos. Over the continental shelf off northwest Europe, upwelling is also caused by winds from the land and the offshore flow of relatively light fresh water from rivers.

distributed food over wide areas of sea. In temperate regions such as Britain and western Europe and subpolar regions like northern Scandinavia and Greenland, thorough mixing leads to high productivity at sea and makes fishing good for both birds and Man. In polar regions, the short summer bringing light and ice-free conditions is accompanied by a sudden and spectacular increase in marine life, and in particular in the planktonic shrimp krill which forms the basis of very nearly all food chains. Seabirds, whales and seals all time their breeding seasons to coincide with this abundance of food.

2 How the birds cope

Life in a coastal habitat offers birds both advantages and disadvantages. The most essential requirement is the maintenance of a food supply. Although masses of suitable food is available in intertidal muds, for example, the birds' behaviour and body design or morphology has to be adapted to exploit it. On mudflats they feed mainly at low tide and several hours either side of it and roost at high tide when the sea covers their foraging areas. They must learn how and where to find food and also have the means of extracting it from beneath the mud's surface. The other coastal habitats present similar problems. Food is not always equally abundant and sometimes it is not available to the birds. For example, cold weather may drive invertebrates deep into the mud, or the most abundant invertebrate species present may be unsuitable as prey for the birds. The birds must be able to cope with both temporary food shortages and more long-term changes in feeding conditions which may even necessitate migration.

The birds which breed at the coast need to find a safe place in suitable nesting habitat free from disturbance and preferably from predators for the duration of the breeding season. They require extra food to form eggs and feed the chicks. For seabirds, which usually forage over wide areas of ocean, this presents a special problem as the breeding season is the only time in the year when they are tied to the land. Other difficulties associated with nesting, such as finding and keeping a mate and breeding successfully, are shared by birds in every other major habitat.

The constantly changing habitats on the coast make it advantageous for birds to be flexible in their behaviour. Areas rich in food one winter may be barren the following year, if local conditions change during reclamation for example, or water in a lagoon may rise and submerge shingle islands used for nesting. Predators are a threat to birds everywhere at all times of the year, but particularly during the breeding season when large numbers of birds gather together to nest. Waders which are perfectly camouflaged on the nesting grounds become conspicuous when feeding on open mudflats, despite their change to non-breeding plumage. Seabirds are comparatively safe at sea but risk predation when they come ashore.

Another problem associated with life on the coast is the extreme saltiness of the environment. Birds which breed on fresh water inland must be able to adjust their physiology to cope with high salinities when they visit the coast. Seasonal temperature changes also have to be tolerated, including both heat and cold, and either can affect the birds' food supply. Feathers, essential for insulation, flight and other functions, are meticulously maintained by preening; they also need thorough waterproofing and replacement at regular intervals. Birds adapt to life in and near salt water in a number of ingenious ways and the lengths to which they go depend mainly upon how much time they spend there. Some species visit the coast only by accident during migration, some do so every autumn or winter, whilst others spend all their lives there. Seabirds which divide their time between land and sea must also change their habits accordingly.

Birds have adapted to cope with their environment by the process of natural selection during their evolution. Certain structures or habits, which arise almost by accident at first, are such an advantage to the individuals possessing them that these birds are able to leave more offspring also possessing the same characteristics. In this way successful traits are favoured by natural selection whilst weak or useless features are gradually eliminated. The usual adaptations in birds affect either their morphology or their behaviour or both.

All birds are primarily adapted for flight which is of major importance in their design but coastal birds have a number of special adaptations. In some species wings are also used for propelling the birds underwater and this is best shown in the auk family, paralleled by the diving petrels and flightless penguins of the southern hemisphere. The wings of a Puffin, for example, are short and broad, so short in fact that the bird is almost unable to glide and quite incapable of agile manoeuvres in flight. The auks find taking off and alighting on land or sea difficult, especially if there is no head wind to give them lift. They are perfectly designed, however, for underwater swimming where the wings are used as flippers to drive the body forwards. Here they are agile and even graceful in contrast to their performance on land. In one species, the Great Auk, the wings were so reduced that the birds were completely flightless and, although experts underwater, they were helpless on land. So many Great Auks were slaughtered by Man for food that the species became extinct in the middle of the last century. Divers, grebes and Cormorants swim underwater and their wings, although not used in swimming, are typically short and broad.

Wings are also modified for different types of flight (see figure 17). The petrels, which include the Fulmar and shearwaters, have characteristically long, narrow wings. Most of the elongation is in the inner part of the wing; a shearwater has about twenty-five secondary wing feathers, compared with sometimes as few as twelve in a duck. Petrels' wings are specially designed for gliding flight which enables them to cover vast distances at sea using the minimum amount of energy. This is essential for they rely on a scattered food supply which requires a huge foraging area. Other birds which glide over land, like eagles and buzzards, take advant-

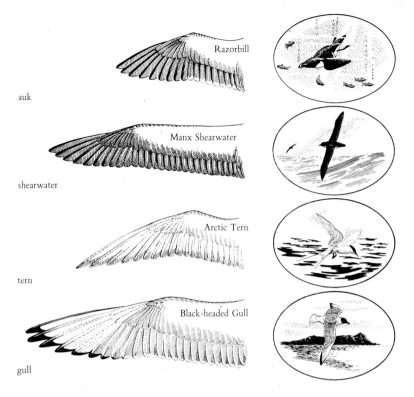

Figure 17 Wings are adapted for different types of flight although they all follow the same basic pattern with the primary and secondary feathers attached to the outer and inner wing bones respectively. In the rounded auk wing, the outer primary feathers are nearly of equal length, and the wing is ideally shaped for underwater propulsion. The shearwaters' elongated wings are due to the large number of secondary feathers and enable the birds to undertake effortless long-distance gliding flight. The long outer primaries in the terns' wings allow the birds to hover and manouevre accurately whereas the strong, broad gulls' wings are more suitable for direct short-distance flights.

age of warm air currents or thermals rising high above the ground. Petrels use air currents above the surface of the sea in a similar way. By heading into the wind, they are lifted without the effort of flapping and they then turn and glide downwards to the water's surface. This is why shearwaters seen at sea glide close to the surface in a rising and falling path. The terns' pointed wings are adapted for the precisely controlled flight needed for hovering and plunge-diving straight into water. The waders also have long, pointed wings and, like the terns, they need these for long-distance migratory flight. Other coastal birds such as wildfowl, Grey Heron and most gulls have strong, broad wings which are used for powerful direct flight.

The shape of the body of many birds reflects the ways in which they

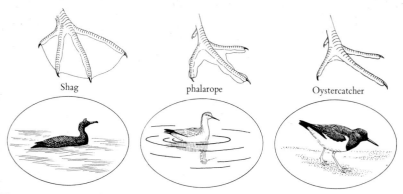

Figure 18 Most coastal birds have three forward-pointing toes and the fourth is vestigial or absent, as in the Sanderling and auks. In diving species like Cormorants and Shags the feet are set well back and the toes webbed for maximum propulsion. In birds which both swim and wade, like phalaropes, partial webbing is adequate and in waders no webbing at all is needed.

move. Wide-ranging birds – the waders, terns and petrels – have slim, compact bodies. Species like divers, grebes and auks have streamlined, elongated bodies with short rudder-like tails. The legs and feet, which are adapted for swimming in these species, are set far back in a position where they can drive the body through the water like propellers. All diving species use their legs and feet for underwater swimming except the auks which use their wings. The legs are often laterally flattened to reduce water resistance and act like paddles; the toes are webbed. Birds which swim on the surface, like ducks and gulls, have webbed feet

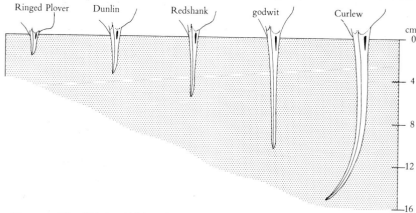

Figure 19 The differing bill lengths in waders enables them to remove food from the same area of mud without competition. The long-billed Curlews and godwits probe deeply for burrowing worms, while the shorter-billed Redshanks and Dunlin collect invertebrates from nearer the surface. Sandpipers and plovers pick food from the surface or just below it.

although waders can swim successfully without webs, and both phalaropes, which have only partly webbed toes, and grebes, which have lobed rather than fully webbed toes, are strong swimmers (see figure 18).

The shape of the bill and, to a lesser extent, the skull is related to the method the bird uses to obtain its food. The various species of waders avoid competing with one another for food by removing different kinds of prey from varying levels in the same area of mud, using bills which cover a whole range of different shapes and lengths (see figure 19). The structure of the bill is similarly adapted to diet in other coastal species. The shearwaters, which feed on large fish, have narrow but surprisingly strong and sharp bills, whilst the much smaller and mainly planktonivorous storm petrels have tiny stout bills. Amongst the wildfowl, the Shoveler which sieves invertebrates from the water, the Eider Duck which collects crabs and other prey needing a firm grip, the Teal which dabbles in shallow water or picks up seeds on land, and the Brent Goose which lives by grazing seaweed, all show appropriate bill shapes. Auks, unlike most other seabirds, bring whole fish back to the nest site to feed their chicks. The palate and tongue surface is spiked and ridged in a pattern which varies according to species in order to hold the slippery fish. The Red-breasted Merganser and Goosander, sometimes known as sawbills, also have tooth-like projections on the inside of their bills to hold fish. Some of these examples are illustrated in figure 21.

In some species, other parts of the head are modified for feeding.

Figure 20 An adult Gannet, perfectly adapted for plunge-diving from high above the sea. To withstand the impact of the dive, the bill and skull are stout, the plumage especially thick, and air sacs lie under the skin on the breast. The nostrils, which in most other birds open on top of the bill, are closed in the Gannet and secondary openings, visible on the bill below and in front of the eye, are closed by a flap of skin when the birds is underwater. (See also figure 66.)

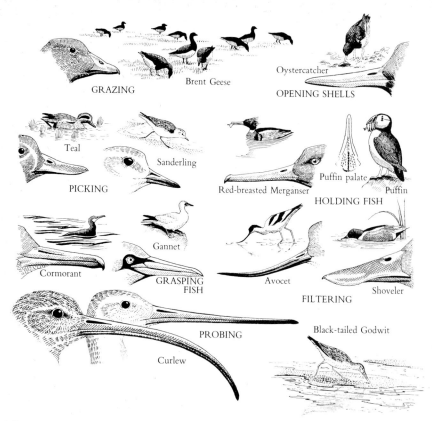

GRAZING

Brent Geese

Oystercatcher

OPENING SHELLS

Teal

PICKING

Sanderling

Red-breasted Merganser

Puffin palate

HOLDING FISH

Puffin

Cormorant

Gannet

GRASPING
FISH

Avocet

FILTERING

Shoveler

PROBING

Black-tailed Godwit

Curlew

Figure 21 This series of drawings illustrates the variety of bill adaptation to diet in coastal species.

Gannets fish by plunging, head first into the sea, rather like terns, from heights of thirty metres or more. They have specially thickened bone in the front of the skull and a stout bill with which to bear the impact of the dive.

In all birds the salt gland is situated in the head at the base of the bill and it is especially well developed in coastal species and others living in salty habitats elsewhere. It removes excess salt from the body by the secretion of an extremely salty, transparent fluid. This drains into the nostrils and can sometimes be seen dripping from the tip of the bill. Gulls reared experimentally in salt-free conditions were found to have poorly developed salt glands, but when they were transferred to a salty environment the gland enlarged. The size and activity of the salt gland is therefore directly related to the habitat in which the bird lives. Not surprisingly, birds which spend much time at sea like petrels, some gulls and auks, all have large salt glands.

The petrels offer us another example of the way in which the body's physiology is adapted to marine life. All species store food in the form of oils rich in fatty acids which are retained in the proventriculus or upper stomach, above the main digestive sack or gizzard. The origin of these oils was much disputed when they were first discovered and their composition bears closest resemblance to the sperm oils found in some species of whales. It now seems fairly certain that the oils are derived from the birds' food and provide a slowly digestible source of energy. This is apparently a special adaptation for the wandering oceanic life led by the petrels. Sometimes, if food is scarce, they are forced to rely on their liquid reserves of proventricular oil. The oil is also given to the chicks at each meal with varying amounts, depending on the chick's age, of partly digested fish and invertebrates. The more solid food is digested quickly, whilst the oils remain in the stomach and provide the chick with a source of nourishment if the parent birds are delayed by bad weather or difficult feeding conditions in returning with the next feed. Both adults and chicks of the petrels, and especially the latter, will spit oil from the stomach as a defence mechanism to deter intruders at the nest. Anyone who has ever approached a Fulmar chick on its nest will know how revolting, smelly and accurately aimed the oil is.

Feathers serve several important functions in coastal birds, in addition to enabling flight and contouring the body into a streamlined shape. Insulation is particularly essential in the cold temperatures experienced on the coast. The wildfowl, petrels, auks and grebes all have thick layers of down below their outer body feathers – hence the difficulty of plucking

Figure 22 A Fulmar, sitting on its nest and single egg, spits oil at an intruder. In the family Procellariideae to which the Fulmar and other petrels belong the nostrils open into long tubes visible on the top of the upper mandible. The family is sometimes referred to as the tubenoses.

a goose. The plumage also needs waterproofing, and a special gland at the base of the tail produces waterproof oil which the bird smears carefully and thoroughly on its feathers whilst preening. The oil gland is particularly well developed in coastal birds but is reduced and nearly absent in the Cormorants and Shags. In these species the lack of waterproofing on the plumage apparently improves diving ability by allowing air trapped between the feathers to escape so reducing buoyancy. Cormorants and Shags cannot thoroughly waterproof their feathers and are therefore often seen sitting out of the water with their wings open while their plumage dries and warms. Warming is especially important for if the

Figure 23 Juvenile Cormorants with their typically mottled plumage. Their waterproofing is inadequate so the birds must dry their wings and warm the body when they come out of the water. Feather maintenance is essential and some of these birds are preening.

outer feathers cannot repel water, the whole body becomes wet underwater and rapidly loses heat when the birds emerge. The Cormorants' black plumage is ideal for the absorption of heat from the sun and for rewarming the body. Overheating is sometimes a problem for coastal birds, though less so in northern Europe than further south. Birds ruffle their feathers to allow air to cool the skin below when they are too hot, and some can flutter the flap of skin on their throat to cool themselves; the latter behaviour is most characteristic of the Cormorants and Gannet and is known as gular fluttering.

Feathers play an important part in courtship. Among coastal birds this is especially true of the ducks, as most other species have similar breeding plumage in males and females. Each species of duck has its own repertoire of courtship displays, accentuated by the colour and crests of the breeding plumage in the drakes. Waders, like ducks, are spectacular in their breeding plumages although males and females are usually almost indistinguishable. Many of the birds seen on the coast in summer, however, are immature non-breeders, and their plumage is rather drab. Other coastal species which lack an actual breeding plumage make minor changes before nesting, such as the development of the crest on the Shag's head, and the brown hood of the Black-headed Gull. Hard parts of the body, the legs, feet, bills and eye rings, often grow brighter in colour during breeding. An ingenious series of experiments, which involved painting the legs and eye rings of certain species of gulls, was able to prove that the birds recognised each other's species, and hence identified potential mates of their own species by the colour of these key parts of the body. An additional advantage of the breeding plumage of certain waders and ducks is that it helps camouflage birds sitting on the nest, and is therefore some protection against predators. In most of the dabbling ducks, for example, the drake's breeding plumage is conspicuous for attracting a potential mate, whilst that of the duck, which incubates

Figure 24 A drake Goldeneye displays to the duck. Unlike land birds, which use mainly song in courtship, the ducks rely on exaggerated postures in which the more conspicuous drake flaunts his plumage to best advantage.

the eggs and cares for the young, is drab brown.

Feathers wear out eventually and worn or damaged ones must be replaced. Most birds moult all their body feathers twice a year in the autumn and spring, and their even more vital flight feathers in the tail and wings usually once only in autumn. The process of moult and the growth of new feathers requires a lot of extra energy and flying may be difficult, especially if several wing feathers are lost simultaneously. Migratory species like waders are forced to pause and feed whilst moulting. Many northern breeding species moult on estuaries around the southern North Sea where feeding is especially rich, and continue southwards to wintering grounds in southwest Europe and Africa. Other waders moult on wintering grounds, and those breeding further south have time to replace their feathers on or near the nesting grounds before starting migration.

The Grey Plover is interesting because it regularly pauses in the middle of its moult, which was discovered when birds from Siberia caught on

Figure 25 An adult Sanderling caught in autumn during its wing moult. The innermost primary feathers have been shed leaving a gap in the centre of the wing. The new, dark-tipped feathers have begun growing, and six old feathers still remain. The tail and most of the body feathers are being replaced at the same time.

the Wash in eastern England were examined. Some Grey Plovers visiting the Wash in autumn start their wing moult too late to complete feather growth before having to move on to winter in west Africa. Why they delay is unexplained as other waders also breeding as far away as Siberia have plenty of time to moult completely on the Wash before migration. These birds replace the first few primaries, starting as usual from the centre of the wing, then stop and migrate in suspended moult with both old and new feathers in the wing. In addition, about a quarter of the birds arriving on the Wash are already in suspended moult having replaced some primaries on the breeding grounds.

Some ducks make special journeys to safe areas with rich feeding just for the purpose of moulting. Nearly all the Shelducks breeding in northwest Europe (about 100,000 birds) visit the German Waddenzee to moult in autumn, leaving the young ducklings behind on the breeding grounds in the care of a few adults which moult locally. Safety from predators is a serious problem for duck when they are moulting; most of them lose all their flight feathers almost simultaneously and for about three weeks they are completely flightless. In many of these species the drakes assume a drab and inconspicuous eclipse plumage while they are unable to fly as camouflage against predators. They can easily be confused

Figure 26 Waders are pushed onto the last available dry land by the advancing tide. Sanderlings and the few Turnstones are dwarfed by the long-legged Redshanks and much larger Oystercatchers. Roosting birds often stand on one leg, like the Redshank in the foreground.

with females or other species at this time.

Auks also drop all their flight feathers at once when they moult after the breeding season. Enormous flocks of Razorbills and Guillemots and their young gather out of sight of land in rich feeding areas for the three to four weeks that the birds are flightless; during this time the young birds are learning to fish for themselves. These flocks, or rafts of moulting auks are especially vulnerable to oil pollution at sea.

There are many examples of how birds in general have adapted their behaviour to cope with their environment and these are described in any standard book on bird biology. Seabirds, however, show special adaptations to life in the coastal habitats. First, the birds' feeding behaviour is adapted to their food. This is especially important as the variety of feeding methods used by birds on the coast allows many different species to share a habitat without competing for food.

The way in which a bird collects food depends on the kind of food it takes and where this is found. Coastal birds usually feed by one or more of the following methods. As food is available either on the surface or underwater the birds must dive and swim underwater after fish or swim to the bottom to collect invertebrates. Otherwise, they must pick a large number of very small food items, usually plankton, out of surface waters.

They collect food underwater in three ways: by plunge-diving, dropping head first out of the air into the water, often from considerable heights and completely submerging (Gannet, terns); by making a shallower dive from a lower height above the surface and not fully submerging (shearwaters); and by diving underwater from the surface and swimming actively after the prey, often following it to great depths (divers, grebes, diving ducks, auks). In the first two instances the birds rely on the accuracy and momentum of their dive to propel them towards their prey rather than chasing it underwater.

Food is collected at the surface in two ways: the bird up-ends or 'dabbles', submerging its head and shoulders and seizing the prey underwater (ducks, swans, gulls), (this can also be done in shallow water to feed off the bottom); or it picks food from the water's surface. Some birds land only briefly and lightly on the water whilst doing this (Kittiwakes); some remain on the wing and perhaps patter over the surface with their feet (storm petrels); and others swim about on the water (phalaropes, Fulmars). To feed in shallow water the bird has to wade and either probe the bottom for invertebrates with its bill (waders), or sweep its bill through the water sifting out small food particles (Avocets, long-billed waders, Shelducks), or trample the bottom, stirring up the invertebrates so that they float to the surface (some gulls, some ducks).

Some birds collect food from the air while on the wing (gulls, some

Figure 27 An Oystercatcher, in full breeding plumage, on its eggs. Both eggs and chicks are cryptically coloured and well camouflaged from predators and humans alike. This bird is actually piping its alarm call.

terns). Swarming insects are a favourite food source and hawking birds fly in circles high above the ground, especially at evening time. Others steal food by chasing birds and forcing them to regurgitate or drop the food they are carrying (skuas, some terns, some gulls), a habit called kleptoparasitism. This is particularly successful during the breeding season when many birds are returning to a colony with food for their young.

Feeding on land requires several different foraging techniques, often used in combination. Some birds probe for invertebrate prey in mud or sand, apparently locating food by sound or the evidence, such as burrow openings or worm casts, left on the surface (waders). Others pick small invertebrates or plant foods up from the ground (plovers) or graze on grass or exposed seaweed (geese, Wigeon). Birds will prise shellfish from the rocks and open the shells (Oystercatcher) or smash them open by dropping them onto a hard surface (some gulls). Certain species are predators both of other birds' eggs and young, and of fully grown birds and small mammals (gulls, skuas, birds of prey). Others are scavengers feeding on natural or artificial waste such as offal and rubbish (gulls, Fulmars, some waders).

Feeding habits and diet are adapted to the birds' environment and the cycle of roosting and feeding behaviour following the tidal rhythm already described for waders is one example of this. Many waders nest inland where they feed on insects and their larvae and other terrestrial invertebrates whilst breeding. They switch to marine food when they visit the coast on migration and during the winter. Gulls are notoriously adaptable in their choice of feeding methods and foods. Stomach contents from Herring Gulls, for example, collected at a rubbish tip where they were scavenging included broken glass and a ham sandwich in a plastic bag! Kittiwakes, by comparison, are the most pelagic of gulls and also relatively conservative in diet, although in the past seventy years they have taken to scavenging behind fishing boats at sea and, more recently, on urban waterfronts. If weather conditions make fishing difficult during the breeding season, they are unable to adapt their behaviour to feed on alternative prey and many either fail to breed or have little success in rearing young. This happened in 1975 on the Lofoten Islands off northern Norway where none of the 25,000 pairs of Kittiwakes which normally nest on the island of Vedøy laid eggs.

Mobility and adaptability are important if birds are to locate and exploit food supplies on the coast. As conditions often vary seasonally, many species have developed the endurance and navigational skills required for migration. Food is usually available in almost unlimited supply on the nesting grounds whilst the birds breed, but conditions often deteriorate soon afterwards. This is especially true for waders and wildfowl and seabirds breeding in the High Arctic of Canada, Greenland and Siberia where the 'summer' is very short. The birds migrate southwards, often stopping off on the coasts of western Europe which offer many suitable habitats. Some move as far south as west Africa to spend the winter on rich feeding grounds. In spring they feed up again for the northward journey to the nesting areas.

The migration patterns of the species found on the coast are described in more detail in Chapter 3. Most of the birds seen on the coast in autumn and winter are migrant visitors, and migration plays an important part in the life of many birds. One pattern of migration, found in several species of waders, involves 'leap-frogging' by different subspecies, possibly to avoid straining the resources of any single wintering area. Turnstones, for example, which breed in northern Scandinavia, visit the estuaries in Britain and Ireland on migration. These birds belong to the subspecies *Arenaria interpres morinella*, and they pause only briefly to feed and moult on the Wash and elsewhere before continuing south, to winter from Iberia to west Africa. In doing so they overtake the more northerly breeding birds of the subspecies *Arenaria interpres interpres*, which nest in arctic Canada and northeast Greenland, which also migrate to Britain. They moult on estuaries such as the Wash and remain there through the winter.

Among the more spectacular of the long-distance migrants are the Manx Shearwater and the Arctic Tern. The first makes a full circle of the Atlantic on its way to and from wintering grounds off Brazil. The Arctic Tern flies to the Antarctic from breeding grounds in the northern hemisphere as far north as the Arctic. In doing so this species lives through more daylight than any other bird in the world, experiencing the perpetual daylight of both the arctic and antarctic summers, the latter during the northern winter.

Figure 28 A flock of migrant Sanderling and Dunlin. Most migration is carried out in a series of hops, sometimes of many hundreds of kilometres, and the birds usually fly at night. They need to pause and replenish their fat stores during migration, and for this the estuaries of northwest Europe are vitally important.

Migration requires a special energy supply which is provided by the body's deposits of fat. Waders feeding on an estuary in spring are building up food stores before migrating. Many species pause to feed in Europe, especially the west coasts of Britain and Ireland, during spring before making the last leg of the journey to their northern breeding grounds. For waders breeding in the High Arctic it is particularly important that they should arrive in good condition. The snow-free conditions of summer are of fairly short duration, and the birds have to nest and lay eggs soon after they arrive. Iceland is used as a stopping off place and feeding ground for Sanderling, Knot and Turnstones bound for Greenland and Canada. Sanderling can increase their body weight by between three and five per cent per day on the Wash in spring, and nearly double their fat-free weight as a result. Waders are estimated to use up about one per cent of their body weight in flying for an hour at an average speed of 110 kph. The Sanderling leaving the Wash carry enough 'fuel' for non-stop flight if necessary to northeast Greenland or Novaya Zemlya in the USSR where they breed.

Feeding behaviour is also adapted for survival during winter. Cold weather can make conditions difficult for waders and other birds on the coast and often many die. Waders are able to tolerate low temperatures and poor feeding by building up a store of fat beforehand on which to survive cold spells. All species of waders wintering on the Wash have a typical pattern of weight changes between October and March. Weight is gained steadily up to a mid-winter peak in December or early January; fat reserves then decline until weight is at its lowest in early spring. Studies of Dunlin have shown that the fat laid down in the first half of the winter is an insurance against cold weather, but that as cold spells become less and less likely and of shorter duration as the spring approaches, the food store is gradually used up. Extra weight needs extra energy to carry it in flight and it is not worth the birds carrying heavy fat deposits around with them late in the winter when they are unlikely to be needed. It is interesting that Dunlin wintering in Ireland, where average winter temperatures are higher than on the east coast of England and very cold spells are rare, have no peak weight in midwinter. They survive the winter months without requiring extra food stores.

Most of the birds on the coast try to avoid predation by flocking behaviour, taking advantage of the safety in numbers. This relies on the tendency for a predator attacking a flock of birds to be bewildered by the choice of prey and to be less successful at catching any of them. Waders, wildfowl and gulls feed and roost together in large numbers, especially in habitats such as mudflats where they have no other protection against predators. Seabirds often nest at high densities when they come to land to breed, and site their colonies only in places less accessible to predators, such as steep cliffs, islands and remote spits. Colonial nesting also has its disadvantages because such a potential larder obviously attracts predators during the breeding season. The vast colonies of up to a million or more

Little Auks in Greenland support many predators including gulls, skuas, Gyrfalcons, Arctic Foxes and Polar Bears which feed on the eggs and dead birds falling from the cliffs. Terns, gulls and skuas which nest in conspicuous colonies will aggressively attack and even hit intruders, including humans, to the colony.

Figure 29 Few birds will actually hit an intruder at the nest, although this Great Skua has just come very close to it. Gulls, terns and skuas all drive potential predators away from their nests or colonies by piercing screams and dive-bombing or mobbing.

Other species opt for safety in camouflage whilst breeding. The coastal nesting Eider Duck nests solitarily and the plumage of the female almost exactly matches her surroundings when incubating. When approached she crouches low on the nest and freezes in an effective anti-predator reaction.

Figure 30 The dappled brown plumage of the female Eider Duck provides excellent camouflage for her whilst incubating on the down-filled nest. The drake Eider who plays no part in the incubation is conspicuously black-and-white.

The nests and eggs of waders, which also nest solitarily, are extremely well camouflaged and sometimes nearly impossible to find. Among sea-birds the general rule applies that offshore feeding species tend to breed in large, inaccessible colonies, and inshore species breed in smaller colonies at lower nesting densities.

Behavioural adaptations are mainly responsible for the lack of competition for either food or nesting sites between birds breeding together on the coast. For seabirds, the breeding season is the one time that competition for food at sea near the nesting colony could become intense. At all other times of the year the pelagic species at least are not tied to land and can forage over huge areas of sea. In fact the breeding seasons of most seabirds in northwest Europe are timed to coincide with a seasonal abundance of food which occurs in spring and summer. This is caused by the life-cycles of the marine plankton and fish which spawn seasonally according to the supplies of light and nutrients (see page 16). The super-abundance of food while the birds are breeding helps to reduce competition, and in addition species have specific preferences for certain kinds of prey or sometimes different foraging areas. The four species of auks sharing a colony, for example, mostly take separate food. Black Guille-mots feed on a variety of fish and crustaceans collected from the bottom of the sea just offshore, whilst Guillemots and Razorbills feed close to land; the former take mainly sprats and the latter sandeels. Puffins sometimes forage with the two larger auks but they usually feed on fish far out to sea; they prefer whitebait and sandeels of a smaller average size than Razorbills. Different habitat preferences also reduce competition for nest sites between species of seabirds in a colony and examples of this are given in Chapter 4.

In all stable populations of birds, the number of breeding adults which

Figure 31 A Dunlin's nest in northeast Greenland, with its clutch of four eggs, hidden in the top of a tussock on a coastal swamp. Despite the birds' display flights and song over the nesting territory, the nest itself is difficult to find.

die each year (mortality) exactly balances the number of young birds breeding for the first time (recruitment). The way in which this happens in coastal birds, known as population dynamics, is adapted to life in comparatively difficult conditions. All seabirds and many waders do not breed until they are two or more years old. In pelagic seabirds like the Fulmar and Gannet, the age of first breeding may be six or seven years or even older, whilst in inshore, non-migratory species like the Shag, breeding begins at two or three years of age. This deferred maturity as it is known is thought to be one way in which birds cope with life in a habitat as difficult as the sea. Finding food at sea is often hard and, although the birds' fishing skills probably increase with experience, young birds have an arduous time. Mortality between fledging and breeding age, during which the birds are classed as immatures, is always high. If seabirds were to attempt to breed any earlier in life they would be most unlikely to succeed in finding the extra food essential for breeding. The same is true of waders which have the difficulties of a long-distance migration twice a year to overcome before they breed regularly.

Immature birds often remain in rich feeding areas during the summer and do not return to the colony. Young of the Razorbill and Guillemot, for example, migrate to seas off Iberia and in the case of the Razorbill north Africa, and few return to the breeding colony in their second summer of life. The breeding adults of these species are non-migratory and disperse locally from the colony after breeding; Guillemots re-occupy their colonies occasionally during the winter.

The recruitment of young birds into the breeding population depends on how many of the birds breeding in previous years were successful in rearing young to fledging (breeding productivity), and also on the levels of mortality among immature birds. Both these influence the number of young birds which survive to breeding age. Normally seabirds and, to some extent, waders have very low adult mortality; as a result they are long-lived, ages of more than twenty years being quite common and perhaps only five or ten adults out of every hundred breeding pairs die each year. Relatively few eggs are laid but breeding productivity is high because nesting success is good. One hundred breeding birds might produce twenty or thirty fledged young in a year, but heavy mortality during immaturity reduces these to the five or ten birds of breeding age needed to replace dead adults for the population to remain stable. In this way the numbers are maintained in a delicately balanced equilibrium.

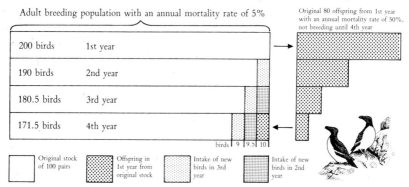

Figure 32 Here the dynamics of a stable seabird population is shown based on a unit of one hundred breeding pairs. These produce eighty fledged young in the first year which are reduced to ten birds by the fourth year when they enter the breeding population. When numbers are stable, these new recruits exactly replace the current annual mortality of adult birds. In this case, the adult mortality is 5 per cent a year so that ten birds die from the original one hundred pairs.

The turnover of generations is considerably faster in a passerine species by comparison. For example, a Blackbird lays four or more eggs and breeds up to three times each season. The potentially large number of offspring is reduced by low nesting success – usually only about half the chicks survive to fledging – and high mortality between fledging and first breeding two seasons later. Mortality of adults is relatively high and at least half the breeding birds in one season die within a year. Many young birds must be produced to replace them if numbers are to remain stable.

A sudden increase in mortality caused by abnormal factors, which unfortunately often originate with Man, can have a disastrous effect on bird populations. Oil pollution incidents at sea, for example, can kill tens of thousands of both breeding adult and immature seabirds at one time. The increase in losses from the breeding population is impossible to counteract by recruitment of immature age groups because many of these have also been killed. The breeding population declines sharply and the resulting lowered annual breeding productivity means that the total numbers of the species will take several years to recover. Fortunately, Man can also have a beneficial effect on bird populations by improving nesting habitats and hence breeding productivity, or by reducing mortality levels. Man's effect on birds is discussed in more detail in Chapter 6.

At present numbers of several of the coastal species are not stable and the most notable of these are the gulls. The growth of the human population in northwest Europe in the last thirty-five years has led to a large increase in the amount of rubbish and sewage being dumped in and around major cities. Gulls, always quick to exploit new food sources by adapting their behaviour, have taken advantage of the opportunity of extra food. Apart from the Kittiwake and Common Gull, all species feed in flocks at rubbish dumps from time to time. The regular supply of food helps many which might otherwise die in cold weather to survive the winter. As a result, gull populations have been increasing rapidly, both in Europe and elsewhere, sometimes to the detriment of other species like terns sharing their breeding colonies, and to the annoyance of some town-dwellers who have to put up with the mess and noise of gulls nesting on their buildings. The Lesser Black-backed Gull, normally a migrant species which visits Iberia and north Africa in winter, has begun to remain in northwest Europe in considerable numbers during winter where it apparently survives by feeding largely on rubbish. The expanses of water in reservoirs and gravel pits in urban areas, the result of supplying water and roadstone for the increasing human population, gives the birds ideal roosting sites close to their food supply. The availability of rubbish food also helps breeding birds to feed their young and in areas where nesting gulls feed on rubbish, sewage or offal from fish factories, breeding productivity is significantly higher than for birds feeding their chicks on more natural, marine foods.

3 Introducing the birds

The first problem for anyone who visits the coast and sees birds there is how to identify them. One can watch and enjoy birds without knowing their names, but if the species can be distinguished, much additional information becomes available by reading and talking to other people about them. A flock of unidentified, medium sized, grey and white birds with long legs and bills may be fairly interesting to watch. When they are known to be waders, they are recognisable as probable visitors from overseas which may be only pausing in this country before continuing their migration. If they are identified as Knot, one knows that they have left their arctic breeding grounds in Canada or Greenland late in the summer, probably replaced their feathers by moulting on the mudflats of the Dutch Waddenzee, and arrived to winter in Britain before returning to the Arctic via Iceland. With experience, other observations can be made which give a further insight into the birds' lives. The more speckled Knot in a flock seen in autumn are young birds, hatched on the tundra only a few months previously. In spring, some of the birds may have tinges of a deep chestnut on their breast feathers; this is the beginning of the splendid breeding plumage they assume in the nesting season. If watched closely, the birds can be seen extracting food from the mud by probing with their bills. On any stretch of mud where waders have been resting or roosting, one can find small pellets containing the indigestible parts of their food. Pellets regurgitated by Knot contain mostly fragments of shell which may be identifiable as belonging to the tellin, their main food species.

With the help of this book you should be able not only to identify most of the birds commonly seen on the coast, but also to discover more about them. Information on their basic appearance, how they behave, what they eat and where they breed and travel on migration is summarised for each species. The habitats they occupy on the coast, and some of the ways in which they are adapted to life there have already been described. There are a number of excellent books published as field guides or handbooks for the identification of birds. These specialise in descriptions and illustrations of every species, with details on the different plumages encountered in the field and distribution maps. The use of one or more of these books is strongly recommended for anyone attempting to bird-watch on the coast. A comprehensive list of these and of books covering both seabirds generally and individual species can be found in the Further reading section.

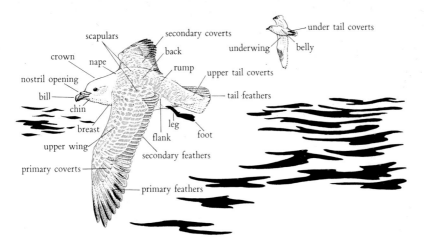

Figure 33 The main parts of the body in a typical seabird. These names are used in the detailed bird descriptions found in field guides.

As well as using books to identify birds, it is a great help to visit the coast with an experienced birdwatcher. A practised observer can find and identify the different kinds of birds with the most perplexing ease by all sorts of small clues unnoticed at first by the beginner. Curiously enough, the knack of identification eventually becomes almost automatic so that one is usually unaware of consciously working out a bird's species. This may seem exasperating to an inexperienced birdwatcher who often has that feeling of near panic and frustration as an unidentified bird flies across his path! The more you watch birds, whether alone or accompanied, the greater your experience will become, and this is more helpful than any number of books or powerful binoculars for identifying birds accurately.

Naming birds

Every species of bird has two names, an English or vernacular name and a Latin scientific name. This may seem complicated but it is essential. English names are sometimes ambiguous; different species may have the same name in different parts of the world and vice versa. For example, the name Fairy Tern applies to both *Gygis alba*, also called the White Tern, and to *Sterna nereis*. Some species have more than one English name; the Spotted Redshank (pictured on the cover) is also known as the Dusky Redshank, and the Dunlin is called the Black-bellied Sandpiper in North America. Each species' Latin name, however, is unique and can be used to identify a species positively. There is the added advantage that Latin names can be understood by ornithologists and birdwatchers of any nationality whether or not they speak your own language.

The system of scientific nomenclature in use today was originally

47

devised by the Swede Linnaeus in 1758. It is called binomial nomenclature because every species has two or more Latin names. The same system is applied to all plants and animals discovered in the world, including fossil species. A similar binomial nomenclature is also used for cloud formations.

Linnaeus' system gives names to each species and also classifies them by grouping according to their evolutionary affinities. Organisms descended from a common ancestor are more closely associated than others which may look very similar because of parallel or convergent evolution, but which actually have a different ancestry.

Birds belong to the class *Aves* and this is divided into about twenty-nine orders (taxonomists disagree on the exact number) of which ten concern us here. Each order contains one or more families; species in the same family are more closely related than those belonging to the same order. The names of orders and families are easily separated by their endings; orders end in *-iformes* and families in *-idae*. The species of birds commonly occurring on the coast of northwest Europe are classified as follows:

Order	Family	Number of coastal species in family	English name of species
Gaviiformes	Gaviidae	4	divers
Podicipitiformes	Podicipedidae	5	grebes
Procellariiformes	Procellariidae	6	petrels
Pelecaniformes	Sulidae	1	gannets
	Phalacrocoracidae	2	cormorants
Ardeiformes	Ardeidae	1	herons
Anseriformes	Anatidae	20	wildfowl
Falconiformes	Falconidae	2	falcons
	Accipitridae	1	hawks
Charadriiformes	Haematopodidae	1	oystercatchers
	Charadriidae	26	waders
	Recurvirostridae	1	avocets
	Phalaropididae	2	phalaropes
	Stercorariidae	4	skuas
	Laridae	16	gulls and terns
	Alcidae	6	auks
Columbiformes	Columbidae	1	pigeons

Passeriformes	Alaudidae	2	larks
	Corvidae	4	crows
	Motacillidae	2	pipits
	Sturnidae	1	starlings
	Fringillidae	3	finches

Within each family the different species are grouped into genera (singular: genus) and every species is known in Latin by its generic and specific names, rather in the way that, in Britain, everyone is called by a surname (shared with their closest relations) and a Christian name (their own but not necessarily unique). Thus the Latin name of the Razorbill is *Alca torda* and it is the only existing member of the genus *Alca*. Some species, but by no means most, are further subdivided into subspecies. This is especially important in certain waders where different subspecies have separate breeding distributions and migration patterns, for example, Turnstones, Dunlin, and Sanderling. The scientific name for the subspecies of Dunlin found nesting in Britain is thus *Calidris alpina schinzii* (genus: *Calidris*; species: *alpina*; subspecies: *schinzii*), and this is replaced by the subspecies *Calidris alpina alpina* (*C.a.alpina*) in winter when birds breeding further north visit Britain. The English name of a species usually applies to all subspecies.

The coastal species

The descriptions that follow are designed to help recognition of the birds commonly seen on the coast. Birds are obviously very mobile, and nearly every species occasionally turns up unexpectedly far outside its usual geographic range or habitat. This is especially true of migratory species, particularly waders and seabirds, which are often blown off course by gales and storms. Almost any species of bird living in northern Europe, and many of those from North America and Asia, may be seen on the coast at some time or another but this book is concerned only with the regular coastal species. A few of the birds included have relatively restricted ranges in northwest Europe but quite often visit the coast outside their range in small numbers.

The species are grouped according to the orders listed above. The groups are introduced by a general statement on typical appearance and approximate size with the body length given in centimetres. Details of exact plumage, characteristics and measurements for each species in the group can be found in any of the field guides mentioned in the Further reading section. Information on the birds' behaviour, calls, typical range and their status on the coast is given here, the latter with special reference to Britain and Ireland and the surrounding seas. The term 'accidental' is used to refer to species infrequently recorded in small numbers on the coast of northwest Europe, and 'rare' to species regularly recorded in small numbers. 'Common' refers to species which often occur on the coast in either large or small numbers.

Divers

Heavily built, long-necked birds with torpedo-shaped bodies and short, pointed wings; rarely seen out of water. Body size similar to small goose 50–85 cm. Plumage basically black above and white underneath.

Black-throated Diver

Short legs and webbed feet set far back on body to aid swimming; shuffle clumsily on land. Swim on surface of water with body nearly awash, sometimes only the head emerges. Can dive effortlessly from surface, submerging without a ripple and remain underwater for a minute or more at a time. Take to wing after laboriously flapping along water surface paddling with feet. Slow wing beats, outstretched neck, stout pointed bill and body shape are characteristic in flight; feet project beyond short tail. Eerie wailing calls, especially on breeding ground. Sexes similar in appearance, but separate breeding 'summer' and non-breeding 'winter' plumages. Young birds often paler than adults. Shape and colouring of head and bill important in distinguishing species. Nest very close to water on lakes and pools and slow rivers, sometimes far inland. Visit the coast, usually estuary mouths and sheltered waters, outside the breeding season. Feed on fish. Divers known as loons in North America.

White-billed Diver Distinguished by large size 85 cm and uptilted pale coloured bill. Breeds on coast in northeast Norway; accidental south of central Norway.

Great Northern Diver 70–80 cm Separated from previous species by black bill and from following two by black head in summer and short thick neck. Identification difficult in winter. Breeds in Iceland, rare visitor to other European coasts in winter.

Red-throated Diver 55 cm and **Black-throated Diver** 60–68 cm Breed throughout northern Europe; common in small numbers on estuaries and inshore waters during winter. Migrate along coast, usually flying high, Black-throated Divers sometimes in flocks. Both species often form flocks in winter. Red-throated has uptilted bill, and Black-throated straight.

Grebes

Long-necked, swimming and diving birds, rarely seen in flight. Vestigial tail and lobed toes for swimming. Large species like Great Crested Grebe are similar in body size to small duck 40–45 cm, smallest, the Little Grebe, is about half this size. Generally distinguished on water

Great Crested Grebe

from rather similar divers by smaller size and more upright neck position although divers also raise necks if alarmed.

Agile swimming and diving; skulking habits on breeding grounds. Wailing and trilling calls. Sexes similar in appearance but special breeding plumage marked by head plumes forming crest or 'ears'. (These and the satiny feathers from breast once highly valued by milliners.) Shape and colouring of bill, head and neck important in distinguishing the species **Great Crested**, **Red-necked**, **Slavonian**, **Black-necked** and **Little Grebes** (in descending order of size). All breed in northern Europe; elaborate courtship involving displays or 'water dances' in the Great Crested. Build floating nests on inland lakes and pools; young often carried on parent's back after leaving nest. Visit coasts, especially sheltered waters, in winter. Sometimes solitary, also form large mixed-species of flocks at traditional sites. Local migration along coast chiefly to avoid cold weather is undertaken largely by northern birds moving on wing at night, often by moonlight, and swimming during day. Red-necked Grebes accidental to south and west of Britain and Channel. Feed on fish and small invertebrates. Eat own feathers and feed them to chicks. These form a lump in the stomach apparently aiding digestion.

Petrels

Oceanic seabirds living mostly far from land and coming ashore only to breed. Long, narrow wings adapted for gliding rather than flapping flight. Bills deeply grooved and hooked, with conspicuous nostril openings – hence the name 'tubenoses' often applied to the group. Body size of Fulmar and shearwaters

Manx Shearwater

approximately that of small duck 35–47 cm, and storm petrels (smallest known seabirds) sparrow-sized 15–20 cm. Plumage basically white below and grey (Fulmar) or black above, except for Sooty Shearwater which is black all over. Both storm petrels and Great Shearwaters have white rumps.

Apart from Fulmar, European petrels are almost always seen only at sea, sometimes far from land. Characteristic gliding flight with wings held stiffly outstretched, rarely flapping. Sweep close to surface of water and often follow in the wake of a ship at sea. Shearwaters and Fulmar will settle on the surface to feed; storm petrels feed from the surface whilst in flight by pattering with feet. Shearwaters also make shallow dives from the surface and swim underwater. Sometimes have difficulty in taking off from water in windless conditions. Storm petrels and shearwaters have extraordinary croaking calls, heard mainly in the breeding colony at night or occasionally at sea. Fulmar uses cackling calls at colony. Sexes similar in appearance, no breeding plumage. Size and markings on upper surface important in distinguishing species. Feed on fish and zooplankton near sea surface. Shearwaters specialise in finding shoaling fish such as sardines, herring and anchovies, whilst storm petrels and Fulmar feed mainly on plankton. Fulmar also scavenges rubbish and offal behind ships at sea which may be partly responsible for its phenomenal population increase this century (see page 139). Petrels have a habit peculiar to their order of spitting foul smelling oil at intruders approaching the nest site. This ability is especially well developed in Fulmar and other seabirds hit by Fulmar oil can be totally incapacitated and die.

Manx Shearwater 35 cm Breeds in Britain, Ireland, Faeroes and Iceland, nesting in burrows on cliffs or offshore islands. Active at colony only by night. Trans-equatorial migration in loop around Atlantic, wintering off Brazil. Common in coastal waters during autumn; can be seen from projecting headlands whilst seawatching (see page 120). Also flocks in rafts on water near colonies during evening in breeding season.

Storm Petrel and **Leach's Petrel** 15–20 cm Distinguished by tiny size and flitting, swallow-like flight. Leach's Petrel has forked tail and feint wing bars. Breed in rock cracks and crevices, usually on offshore islands; Storm Petrels in Britain, Ireland, Norway and Iceland; Leach's Petrel restricted to a few islands off northern Scotland, Faeroes and one site off northern Norway. Disperse into Atlantic after breeding. Seen from land only very rarely, usually after stormy weather, although common in small numbers offshore and can be seen from ships at sea.

Great Shearwater and **Sooty Shearwater** 42–46 cm Rare visitors to coasts of northwest Europe from breeding colonies in south Atlantic. Similar shape to Manx Shearwater but larger. Great Shearwater has white rump and nape, black cap and greyish mantle; lacks black tips to underwing which are typical of Manx Shearwater. Sooty Shearwater is black with pale centres to underwings. Both seen offshore especially whilst seawatching in autumn.

Fulmar 47 cm The only petrel in Europe which visits land by day. Nests on cliff ledges around most of coastline of northwest Europe. Non-migratory but disperses locally to sea after nesting, reoccupies colonies before winter. Can be confused with similar sized, pale grey mantled gulls but separable by narrower wings and gliding flight. Also when close by notice large dark eye and prominent nostrils on top of bill. A curious bird which often repeatedly sweeps down close to people on clifftops.

Cormorants and Gannet

Heavily built, stout-billed seabirds, specialised at diving and swimming underwater. Legs far back on body but the birds stand upright on land.

Figure 34 Little Terns can be distinguished easily from other terns by their small size and fast wing beats or by the white forehead and yellow bill when seen close to. Shingle or sandy beaches where Little Terns prefer to nest are often unintentionally disturbed by humans so that breeding success is low.

Strong flight, often in goose-like V-formation when moving to and from feeding grounds. Raucous, croaking voices, heard mainly at breeding colony. Sexes similar in appearance.

Cormorant 90 cm and **Shag** 76 cm Similar in size to divers but distinguished mainly by larger size and all-black plumage. Juveniles are brown-backed with pale undersurface and more white on face than adults. During breeding season Shag grows small crest of feathers on head visible only when raised and

Cormorant

Cormorant has distinct white patch on flanks behind wing. Swim on surface and dive easily to depths of ten metres or more. Broad, pointed wings and fast, shallow wing beats. Main foods are fish and marine invertebrates collected from sea bottom especially off rocky shores. Breed on coasts of northwest Europe and disperse locally after breeding; young birds tend to move further away from the colony than adults. Never far from land and winter in estuaries and inshore seas. Cormorants sometimes fish in flocks of over a hundred birds especially in autumn; this may enhance fishing success. Both species characteristically sit on rocks or other perches near sea with wings outstretched, apparently to dry and warm plumage.

Gannet 91 cm Mainly white with conspicuous black wing tips and yellowish tinged head. Young birds are completely brown with black wing tips but become steadily paler with age as the plumage is suffused with white. Full adult plumage attained at age of five or six years. Fishes by plunge-diving (see page

Gannet

109), often spectacularly from heights of thirty to forty metres or more. Also sits on surface of sea. Nests colonially on cliffs or summit of islands and occasionally on mainland cliffs. Restricted distribution in Britain: fourteen colonies; Ireland: four colonies; Iceland: seven colonies; and Norway: four colonies; also Canada: six colonies. Migrates to sea off west Africa during winter. In autumn common offshore in large numbers and visible from land.

Figure 35 A Herring Gull (above) calls to protect its newly hatched chick still in the nest. The nestling down is fluffy and speckled, but before fledging the young birds assume a streaked pale brown juvenile plumage which is gradually lost during the first three or four years of life. The adult Great Black-backed Gull (below) is accompanied by an immature bird in its second year of life.

Heron

Single species **Grey Heron** 90 cm sometimes incorrectly called a Crane. Common in estuaries and intertidal zone of rocky shores in northwest Europe. Tall, long-necked and long-legged bird with grey plumage and large yellowish bill. Body size similar to large goose; general appearance unique. Short rounded wings,

Grey Heron

flapped slowly in flight with head sunk onto shoulders and legs extended behind tail. Often mobbed by other birds in flight. Feeds on fish and other aquatic prey which are stealthily stalked; often stands motionless waiting for food to approach before striking. Loud, hoarse croaking call. Breeds colonially, nesting in trees usually near water inland throughout west, central and southeast Europe; visits coasts in winter. Sexes similar.

Wildfowl

Water-loving birds with elongated bodies, rounded wings and webbed feet. Swans and geese are large and long-necked. Body size varies from swans 120–150 cm, to geese 55–60 cm, and ducks 35–60 cm. Voices are a whole range of quacks, whistles and honks usually heard in flight. Sexes usually dissimilar in ducks – drakes are more colourful than ducks – and similar, except for size, in other groups. Young birds usually less conspicuously marked and often paler than adults; young swans (cygnets) are brown. Fly in V-formations or skeins, with necks characteristically outstretched. Swans distinguished by their size, heavy flight and all-white plumage. Spread feet out to meet water when coming in to land. Nests are substantial and often lined with down. Clutches of four to ten eggs are normal, and the chicks leave the nest immediately after hatching.

Swans

Mute Swan 152 cm Breeds throughout west and central Europe, usually on fresh water but occasionally on estuaries. Winters in flocks on estuaries and sheltered coastal waters. **Bewick** 122 cm and **Whooper Swans** 152 cm are visitors from breeding grounds in northern Russia and Iceland, or northern Finland

Mute Swan

respectively. Winter in flocks on estuaries and coastal fields, also inland. Species separated from Mute Swan by size and shape with longer neck and flatter body in the water; distinguished from each other mainly by colour and pattern of bill markings.

Geese

Brent 55–60 cm and **Barnacle
Geese** 60–65 cm The only species
regularly seen on coast although
other species occur there sometimes,
especially on coastal fields. Barnacle
Geese breed on inland cliffs in
northeast Greenland and on the
arctic islands of Spitsbergen and
Novaya Zemlya; visit Scotland,

Brent Goose

Ireland and Waddenzee in winter. Feed on grass from saltings, machair,
dune slacks and coastal fields, also on offshore islands and stack tops.
Brent Geese visit estuaries and mudflats of north and west Europe in
winter; dark-bellied subspecies breeds in Siberia, and the pale-bellied in
Spitsbergen and Greenland, wintering almost exclusively in Ireland.
Feed mostly on eel grass growing on mudflats in estuaries. Brent and
Barnacle Geese separated by pattern of plumage and head colour.

Ducks

Fifteen species occur regularly on the
coast and most other species do so
occasionally or as vagrants. Usually
seen swimming or paddling in water.
The colour and pattern of the
plumage, especially wing markings when seen in flight, are useful
identification features as are relative
sizes and silhouettes when seen on

Mallard

water. Watch out for drakes in eclipse plumage which closely resembles
that of female and is easily confused with other species.

Feeding habits can be used to separate species broadly. Diving ducks
submerge readily from the surface (never plunge-dive), but must run
with wings flapping to take off. These include the true 'seaducks'
Common Scoter 45–50 cm, **Velvet Scoter** 50–55 cm, **Eider** 60–65
cm and **King Eider** 55–62 cm which occur in coastal seas and estuary
mouths. Common Scoter nest in Britain, Ireland and northern Scandinavia, and Velvet Scoter in northern Scandinavia and around the Baltic.
Both are common in flocks of up to several hundred on the coasts of
northwest Europe in winter; latter rare in west Britain and Ireland. The
Eider nests beside estuaries, in sand dunes and on offshore islands in
northern Britain, northern Ireland and Scandinavia, and the King
Eider in northern Russia. Both winter in the mouths of estuaries and
inshore waters of northwest Europe but King Eiders are rare south of
northern Scandinavia and Iceland. Other diving duck include **Scaup** 48
cm, **Goldeneye** 45 cm, **Long-tailed Duck** 40–60 cm, **Red-breasted
Merganser** 50–60 cm and **Goosander** 60–70 cm which breed in

northern Europe and move south and west to winter on the coast. Diving ducks feed on fish, crustaceans, molluscs and other invertebrates which they collect mostly from the bottom.

Dabbling ducks feed by up-ending on the surface and jump into the air, without running, when taking off. These are the **Wigeon** 45 cm, **Mallard** 58–60 cm, **Teal** 35 cm, **Pintail** 55 cm and **Shoveler** 50 cm. All are common in huge flocks inland as well as on the coast in winter. The **Shelduck** 60–70 cm not strictly a dabbling duck, never leaves the coast, and often feeds out of water with Wigeon, grazing vegetation on salt-marsh or mudflats. The others dabble for invertebrates in very shallow water or from the surface in deeper water; they also feed on seeds from saltmarsh vegetation. Wigeon are probably the most easily recognised because of their characteristic whistling voices. The dabbling ducks have a widespread breeding distribution in northern Europe, although the Shelduck nests only in dunes, on saltmarsh and on offshore islands.

Other ducks occasionally seen on the coast are **Steller's Eider** (accidental), **Tufted Duck**, and from Iceland **Barrow's Goldeneye** and **Harlequin**.

Hawks and falcons

These birds of prey, or raptors, are the top predators in coastal food chains and they feed on other birds and small mammals. They are slim bodied with small heads, hooked bills, pointed wings, wedge-shaped tails (when spread), and taloned toes. Flight is swift and agile, often with long glides or hovering. Staccato calls. Only two species of the large and varied family Falconidae commonly occur on the coast, although other species may be encountered whilst on migration.

Kestrel 34 cm Smallest of the coastal raptors. Females are larger than males with brown rather than chestnut backs. Underneath buffish and streaked, young birds heavily barred, and otherwise like females. Hovers characteristically whilst hunting, remaining absolutely stationary for a minute or more at a time. Drops onto prey in near-vertical swoop. Nests extensively throughout Europe, in trees, on cliffs and buildings.

Peregrine ♂ 40 cm, ♀ 50 cm Upperparts greyer than Kestrel's; larger size and faster flight also distinctive. Young birds brownish above and barred underneath. Feeds mainly on other birds, especially Rock Doves and waders on the coast, which are caught unawares in flight by a plunging dive at great speed from high above. Impact is often sufficient to decapitate prey. Peregrine then uses special perch whilst removing feathers and eating breast muscles of the kill. A scattering of feathers and half-eaten, often headless corpse are typical marks of a Peregrine plucking post. Nests on inaccessible cliffs throughout Europe, especially on coasts; scarce in southern Britain. Population declined after widespread use of agricultural pesticides, particularly those containing organochlorine compounds, in 1950s and 60s and through excessive egg collecting. The former contaminated the birds' food and caused them to lay thin-shelled eggs which drastically reduced breeding success. Legislation for the protection of birds and control in the use of pesticides has helped to rectify the situation during the last decade.

White-tailed Eagle 68–97 cm The largest bird of prey on the coast and the only hawk, family Accipitridae, to breed there regularly. Pale brown with paler head and white tail, although many young birds are uniformly dark brown. Wings broad and square ended with widely separated primaries easily visible in flight. Nests on cliffs and wooded islands in north and east Europe; rare or accidental in west and south Europe. Once more widespread, bred in Scotland and Ireland but died out because of hunting, egg collecting and pollution by toxic chemicals. Attempts are being made to reintroduce White-tailed Eagles to Scotland by rearing young birds in suitable habitat. Feeds on fish, seabirds and carrion.

Other predatory birds which sometimes hunt in coastal habitats are **Montagu's** and **Marsh Harriers**, **Merlin**, **Sparrowhawk** and **Short-eared Owl**.

Waders

Long-legged birds, mostly with long bills; wings are long and narrow and usually pointed. Unwebbed feet, apart from Avocet and phalaropes. Fast, agile flight; characteristic flocking behaviour on coast. Body sizes variable; females usually larger, especially in bill length, than males; main exception is Ruff. Distinct

Dunlin

breeding and non-breeding plumages, former tinged with deep, vivid chestnut in many species. Young birds usually more speckled than adults.

Size, length of bill, colour of plumage and presence or absence of conspicuous wing markings are all useful in identifying different species. Calls, usually given in flight, are also most distinctive – piping, trills and whistles. At rest wing pattern often exposed when birds stretch or preen. Breed on coast and inland, many on tundra in arctic and sub-arctic regions. Visit the coast on migration and to winter; flock on estuaries and mudflats where intertidal area is rich in invertebrate foods. Probe or pick prey from surface. Waders are most easily separated broadly by size as follows:

Large waders

Oystercatcher 43 cm Black and white bird with pink legs and straight orange bill, especially bright in breeding season. Noisy, repetitive call. Nests mainly on coast of most of northwest Europe. Young birds, and adults which have been probing in muddy soil, have dark brown bills.

Curlew 60 cm Speckled brown plumage and long down-curved bill. Beautiful mellow call. Nests inland on moors and bogs of central and northern Europe, also Britain and Ireland; migrates to coast of west Europe, and southwards to north and west Africa in winter.

Whimbrel 45 cm Bill and plumage similar to Curlew but separable by call, smaller size and distinct dark stripes on crown. Nests far north on tundra and winters in Iberia, north and west Africa.

Avocet 45 cm Unmistakable black and white bird with upturned bill. Rare away from scattered breeding localities in Britain, Holland, Denmark and southern Europe. Winters in small flocks on estuaries. Feet webbed. Feeds with characteristic scything action, gathering invertebrates from water, similar to behaviour of Shelduck. Prefers shallow pools and lagoons on coast for feeding and nesting.

Black-tailed Godwit 40–44 cm Long straight bill, brown plumage with obvious white wing bar and white base to black tipped tail. Nests in central Europe, east to Britain and Iceland; winters from Ireland south to Iberia and north Africa. Common on estuaries in northwest Europe on migration.

Bar-tailed Godwit 35–40 cm Separable from last species by call, slightly upturned bill, barred rump and feint, inconspicuous wing bars. Nests in northern Scandinavia and Russia; visits Britain and the rest of the European coast in winter.

Medium sized waders

Lapwing 30 cm Black back with greenish tinge, white underparts, chestnut undertail feathers. Head black, crowned with crest not always raised. Wings broad and unpointed. Characteristic call has earned it the name 'Peewit' (also sometimes called Green Plover). Nests inland throughout central and west Europe, and gathers in coastal fields and estuaries in winter, forming huge flocks. Also winters inland. Cold weather causes short-distance migration to west and south.

Grey Plover 28 cm Streaked grey back and white underparts. Black patches in 'armpits' useful in identification. Breeds in High Arctic of Russia, passes through northwest Europe to winter from Britain and Ireland south to north and west Africa. Sometimes occurs singly or in small groups, also in flocks. Prefers to feed on sand or mudflats.

Golden Plover 27 cm Back streaked yellowish golden, aids separation from above species. Breeds inland on moors in northern Europe and winters in flocks inland or on mudflats in southern Europe and north Africa.

Redshank 28 cm Speckled brown back, pale underparts, long red legs and bill with darker tip. Look also for white rump and trailing edge to wings in flight; legs tucked under body when flying. Nests on saltmarsh, inland marsh and bog throughout central Europe, and coastally in Norway, Iceland and Iberia. Migrates in flocks along coast and winters on estuaries southwards to north Africa.

Spotted Redshank 32 cm Distinguished from the last species in winter by pale but not white, streaked patches on wings when in flight; and more speckled back and dusky upper breast. Distinct all-black breeding plumage. Nests in northern Scandinavia and Russia; common in small numbers during winter and on passage in southern Britain, southern Ireland, western France, west Iberia, Italy, north and west Africa.

Greenshank 30–35 cm Greyish plumage, legs and bill. Larger than other 'shanks' with slower wing beats. Nests in northern Europe including Scotland on inland moors, and pauses on estuaries usually in small numbers whilst migrating. Winters in west and south Europe and northwest Africa. Prefers drainage channels and muddy creeks of saltmarsh and mudflats.

Ruff Male 30 cm larger than female 24 cm, called Reeve. Difference led to confusion in early identification and male and female were once considered separate species. Inconspicuous mottled brown plumage in winter but males grow splendid ruff on neck and shoulders and head plumes for courtship in breeding season. Characteristic jerky flight, with shallow wing-beats and obvious white patches either side of dark rump are useful for distinguishing Ruff from other similar-sized waders. Nests in north and northeast Europe, also south Baltic and coasts of southern North Sea; scarce in eastern England. Migrates to coast and winters in west and south Europe and north Africa. Usually seen on salt pans, lagoons and inland sewage farms. Often solitary, rarely seen in flocks of more than ten.

Knot 25 cm Plump, greyish backed wader. Winters in huge flocks on estuaries which wheel and turn in the air resembling a cloud of smoke from a distance. Spring and summer plumage spectacular, with bright chestnut underparts and rich brown flecked back. Nests in high Arctic of Canada, Greenland and Siberia; migrates along coasts of Europe to winter on estuaries in Britain, Ireland, France and Holland; others travel to north and west Africa.

Small waders

Ringed Plover 19 cm Distinct striped head and neck, greyish back and white underparts. Short stout bill and legs. Forages on run, grabbing prey from surface. Nests mainly coastally on beaches in northwest Europe and inland on tundra of Greenland. Winters on estuaries and beaches of west and southwest Europe and north Africa.

Kentish Plover 16 cm Rare in Britain, Ireland and Scandinavia. Distinguished from above species by chestnut crown and dark legs. Breeds on coasts of mainland Europe south of Denmark and in north Africa; winters locally.

Turnstone 23 cm Short, pointed bill. Mottled back with black, brown and white, often bearing traces of chestnut summer plumage. Scuttles among rocks and seaweed whilst foraging, and prefers rocky shores or shingle beaches. Breeds in Scandinavia, Russia and northeast Greenland. Found on coast of west Europe on migration and in winter.

Purple Sandpiper 23 cm Distinguished from Turnstone by greyer plumage and longer bill. Also feeds in flocks on rocky shores. Nests on coasts of Iceland and Norway and winters on coasts of western Europe south of this. Rarely seen in flocks of more than fifty although some large winter roosts have been recorded.

Common Sandpiper 20 cm Brownish back, contrasting strongly with pure white underparts. Medium length bill. Brown smudge on shoulder and habit of bobbing immediately after landing are distinguishing features. Nests inland near water throughout Europe; migrates south to winter in Africa. Also occurs on coast, especially muddy creeks and saltpans; sometimes seen in small flocks.

Green Sandpiper 23 cm Greyish upper plumage, white rump and lack of wing bar are characteristic as is loud call. Breeds in northeast Europe, and winters in south and west Europe, mainly on lakes inland. Solitary birds also occur on coast during migration season, usually at sewage farms or in drainage ditches and creeks.

Wood Sandpiper 21 cm Long legs, pale underwing and speckled back distinguishes Wood Sandpiper from Green. Nests inland in north and east Europe including northern Scotland. Winters in west Africa. Occasionally seen on coast, particularly on mudflats and seaweed banks. Rare in Britain, Ireland and western Europe.

Little Stint 14 cm Tiny wader, forages on run making swift probes into mud with small bill like action of a sewing machine needle. Note streaks in V on back. Nests in northern Norway and Russia and winters in extreme south of Europe and north Africa. Occurs in small numbers at coastal sewage farms and on muddy areas of saltmarsh whilst on migration; never seen in large flocks.

Temminck's Stint 15 cm Paler legs and scalloped back plumage (without V or streaking) separates this species from Little Stint. Otherwise similar in shape, behaviour and habitat preference. Breeds in Norway, northern Scandinavia and Russia; rare in west Europe, winters further south in Africa than Little Stint.

Dunlin 17–20 cm Medium-billed wader characteristically seen in large flocks. Greyish back and white underparts in winter, becoming browner or chestnut backed (depending on subspecies) in summer, with distinct black patch on belly. Nests mainly in coastal marshes or inland in northeast Greenland, Iceland, Britain, Ireland and northwards from the south Baltic. Surprisingly tuneful soaring song on nesting territory. Winters on estuaries from northwest Europe to west Africa.

Curlew Sandpiper 18–21 cm Distinguished from Dunlin by white rump and slightly down-curved tip to bill. Reddish tinge to breast in breeding plumage. Nests in Siberia and winters in Africa; accidental but

regular in small numbers in northwest Europe, usually in autumn.
Sanderling 20 cm Pale grey back; typically runs to and fro on beach at edge of waves whilst foraging. Nests on tundra of Canada, Greenland and Siberia. Migrates along the coasts of northwest Europe to winter on sandy shores and estuaries south from Britain, Ireland and Holland to north and west Africa.

Phalaropes

Red-necked Phalarope

In behaviour phalaropes 18–20 cm fall between waders and the more typical seabirds, although they look most like the former. Breeding plumage is brilliant and winter plumage a dull grey. Have long legs like waders but feet are partly lobed for swimming. Bill is short and sharp, used for picking tiny food items from the water's surface. Use a typical spinning movement, swimming in circles in shallow water to stir up food from the bottom. Nest beside water, often far inland at scattered localities in northern Europe including Iceland and Greenland (both species), Scottish islands and much of Norway and northern Russia (Red-necked Phalarope only). Outside the breeding season phalaropes go out to sea and are regularly seen offshore sometimes in vast flocks. Of special interest when breeding as the male bird incubates the eggs and cares for the young without help from the female. Can also be seen from land, especially on autumn migration, and are found at coastal sewage farms or in lagoons or feeding on banks of weed washed up by the sea. **Red-necked** differs from **Grey Phalarope** by its darker, streaked shoulders and back and dark crown; Grey is uniform grey on its head and back. Both winter off west Africa, in the Persian Gulf and northern Indian Ocean.

Other waders sometimes seen on the coast or coastal sewage farms: **Little Ringed Plover**, **Snipe**, **Broad-billed Sandpiper** and **Dotterel** (northern Scandinavia), **Black-winged Stilt** (southern Europe), and some north American sandpipers like **Pectoral Sandpiper**.

Skuas

Arctic Skua

Large, dark plumaged birds with narrow, pointed wings and elongated central tail feathers. Webbed feet and strong hooked bills. Predators, scavengers and pirates, stealing food from other birds. Body size similar to duck 40–60 cm; loud scolding calls especially on nesting grounds. Sexes similar but young birds more mottled. Breed coastally on moorland or tundra and winter at sea, usually far offshore. Sometimes seen from land, particularly during autumn migration and behind ships at sea. Known as jaegers in North America.

Great Skua 50–60 cm Nests in northern Scotland, Faeroes and Iceland; winters in north Atlantic. Conspicuous white wing patches are characteristic. Fierce predator and scavenger. Also called Bonxie.

Arctic Skua 40–50 cm Breeds in northern Scotland, and on coasts of Iceland, Norway, central Baltic and Russia; winters throughout Atlantic. Agile aerial pursuit of other seabirds, especially terns, to steal food (kleptoparasitism). Dark and light and rarer intermediate plumage phases may confuse identification; more dark than light birds in south of range.

Long-tailed Skua 45–55 cm Breeds on tundra of northern Europe and winters off west Africa. Feeds on small mammals, especially lemmings, on breeding grounds but collects food by kleptoparasitism outside breeding season. Grey back, black cap and very long central tail feathers are characteristic; rare off northwest Europe.

Pomarine Skua 40–50 cm Distinguished from Long-tailed by mottled underparts, paler than Arctic Skua, and long, blunt central tail feathers. Dark and light plumage phases. Nests in high Arctic of Russia and winters off west Africa. Rare off west Europe on migration.

Gulls

White seabirds with grey mantle. Wings broad and tipped with black in characteristic patterns for each species. Legs long and thick, feet webbed. Colour of legs, bill and eye ring also useful in identification of species. About duck to goose size 40–70 cm. Voices loud, harsh calls and variety of softer mewings. Feed

Herring Gull

by predation and scavenging at rubbish dumps, fish factories, sewage outfalls, behind ploughs inland and at similar sites; also feed on fish and invertebrates and sometimes hawk for insects. Breed mostly in large colonies on or near coast and sometimes inland. Winter on coast or inland, roosting in huge flocks near water. Sexes similar except in size; young birds differ in plumage from adults, usually mottled brown. Adult appearance not attained until second or third or even fourth year of life, but birds become progressively lighter in colour with age. When not breeding head often streaked brown which should not be mistaken for oiling on plumage.

Large gulls

Herring Gull 60 cm Breeds mainly near coast of north and west Europe;

winters in south and central Europe. Non-migratory but disperses after breeding. Pale grey mantle, pinkish legs. Accomplished scavenger, and predator at seabird breeding colonies.

Lesser Black-backed Gull 55 cm Nests mostly on the coast but also inland in northwest Europe, and migrates to southern Europe and north Africa for winter. Slate grey mantle, lemon yellow legs and slightly smaller size distinguish it from Herring. Mainly a marine feeder whilst breeding, especially on fish; also a predator and scavenger.

Iceland Gull 60 cm Similar appearance to Herring but without black wing tips. Breeds in northwest Canadian Arctic and winters in Iceland and east Britain; rare elsewhere in Europe.

Glaucous Gull 65–80 cm Similar to Iceland but separated mainly by larger size which equals that of Great Black-backed. Breeds in Iceland, northeast Norway and Russia; winters on coast of Norway and south to Holland. Rare elsewhere in Europe.

Great Black-backed Gull 65–75 cm Dark grey back, yellow legs. This and the previous species are the largest of the European gulls. Fierce predator of mammals and other seabirds and their eggs and young; also feeds on fish and intertidal invertebrates. Scavenger, especially in winter. Non-migratory, winters near breeding grounds on coasts of Scandinavia, Iceland, Britain and Ireland, and also coastally to Iberia.

Small gulls

Kittiwake 45 cm Pale grey mantle, very black wing tips, lemon yellow bill with contrasting red gape, and black legs. Nests on cliffs and sometimes buildings on coasts of Britain, Ireland, northwest France, Denmark, Norway and Iceland. Entirely marine, winters out at sea but commonly seen from land. Forages in large flocks over shoaling fish, sometimes scavenges behind fishing boats. Marine feeder on plankton and small fish. Distinctive call resembling bird's name.

Black-headed Gull 40 cm Recognisable by dark chocolate brown head in summer, and smudges of grey on sides of head in winter plumage; also bright red legs and bill. Wing has distinct white leading edge and dark grey patch at tips on undersurface – useful features to look for when examining small gulls in winter plumage. Nests throughout west and central Europe, often inland; winters in southern Europe and north Africa mainly on coast. Feeds and roosts in huge flocks in winter, usually feeds on invertebrates and sometimes scavenges at rubbish tips, sewage outfalls and behind fishing boats inshore. Tramples on mud in fields to bring earthworms to the surface.

Common Gull 40–45 cm Grey backed gull with yellow bill and legs. White tips to black ends of wings are especially characteristic. Rounded head and large dark eye distinctive, especially when compared with the rather similar Herring Gull. Barking voice earned the Common Gull its Latin name *Larus canus*. Nests throughout northern Europe, often far inland; winters on or near coasts of west and southern Europe. Main food is invertebrates, species depend upon feeding habitat.

Little Gull 28 cm Small size, pale grey mantle including wing tips and dark underwing are main distinguishing marks. Legs red. Black head in breeding plumage. Young Little Gulls, like young Kittiwakes, Black-headed Gulls and some of the accidental species mentioned below, have dark W-shaped mark across wings and black-tipped tail. Nests in eastern central Europe and winters in small numbers in North Sea and off coasts of west and south Europe.

Other gulls occasionally seen on coasts of western Europe are **Mediterranean**, **Slender-billed** and **Audouin's** (Mediterranean area), and **Sabine's** (vagrant from High Arctic).

Terns

Small, slender, short-legged sea-birds with webbed feet and long pointed wings. Pale grey mantle, white underparts and black crown. Easily recognised by agile buoyant flight with slow wing beats; also by habit of hovering, then diving steeply to plunge head first underwater when fishing. Take variety of small

Roseate Tern

fish. Size and bill colour useful in separating species. Noisy with rasping voices or repeated calls. Sexes similar; juveniles and adults in winter have white foreheads. Juvenile plumage also generally more speckled. Rare far from land.

Sandwich Tern 41 cm Feathers of crown form characteristic tuft in breeding season giving square look to back of head. Bill black with yellow tips, legs black. Often draws attention to itself by loud grating calls which carry a long distance. Nests at extremely high densities in scattered colonies on coasts of Britain, Ireland, Holland, Germany, Denmark, southern Sweden and also in southern Europe and north Africa. Migrates along coast to winter off west Africa.

Common Tern 36–40 cm Scarlet bill with black tip and red legs in breeding season. Grey veins and darker tips to outer wing feathers makes opaque patch bordered by dark grey at wingtips. Breeds widely in Europe, both coastally and inland, except for central Scandinavia, France and Spain. Migrates along coast to winter off west Africa.

Arctic Tern 36–42 cm Distinguished from Common Tern by call, longer outer tail feathers which project beyond wingtips when at rest, and darker red bill and legs in breeding season. Transparent underwing, fringed by dark grey trailing edge of wing. Nests in Arctic, and coastally around much of northwest Europe. Spectacular long-distance migrant following coast of Europe and Africa to the Antarctic, and north again via west Atlantic.

Roseate Tern 36–42 cm Very rare with few remaining breeding colonies in northwest Europe although exact cause of decline in last twenty years remains a mystery. Individual characteristics are dark red and black bill and feint rosy tinge to breast and belly in breeding plumage. Long tail and lack of grey tips to outer wing feathers are also useful for distinguishing Roseates from other terns. Breeds at scattered localities in Britain, Ireland and France. Rare migrant on coasts, visits west Africa in winter.

Little Tern 23 cm Tiny size and jerky flight most characteristic. Forehead white, even when breeding; bill yellow with black tip and feet yellow. Dark grey leading edge to upper wing. Breeds on beaches and shingle banks on coasts of most of west and south Europe, and inland in central Europe. Migrates along coast to winter in northwest Africa.

Other terns, more common on fresh or brackish water, but sometimes seen on the coast are **Caspian** 50–55 cm, **Gull-billed** 39 cm and **Black** 23 cm. These feed on aquatic invertebrates and will also hawk for insects; Gull-billed takes small vertebrates such as frogs and lizards.

Auks

Small, stout bodied, black or brown and white seabirds. Webbed feet and flattened legs attached well back on the body for swimming. Wings with white tips to secondaries, short, stiff and pointed for underwater paddling. Ungainly on land and when taking off from water. Fast wing beats and clumsy flight often close

above water; birds often follow one another in long strings. Swim on surface and dive for food, submerging up to a minute or more. Rasping croaky voices, noisy at breeding colony. Nest in colonies usually at high density on cliffs or inaccessible slopes, often on offshore islands. Sexes similar; winter plumage has more white on chin and neck than during breeding season. Size and shape of bill and body distinguishes species. Feed mainly on shoaling fish caught near surface.

Guillemot 42 cm Bill stout and pointed, dark brown. Back black in northern subspecies, brown in southern birds. Crowds onto cliff ledges in huge numbers to nest; breeds on coast of northwest Europe south to northwest Spain and disperses to sea after breeding. Often seen at sea from land, rare far offshore. Watch out for bridled birds with spectacle-like line behind eye, a genetic variation not a subspecies, more common in north of range.

Brünnich's Guillemot 42 cm Distinguished from former rather similar species by black upperparts and stouter bill marked with white line at gape. Breeds in Iceland and northern Norway and Russia, disperses to sea sometimes far offshore in winter. Rare off northern Europe and accidental south of Norway. Guillemots known as murres in North America.

Razorbill 41 cm Thicker, laterally flattened bill with transverse white stripe, and white line from bill to eye separates this species from the guillemots. Different profiles in flight and on water also useful and become obvious with experience. Nests in smaller colonies than guillemots, sites scattered in boulder scree or on cliff ledges often among guillemots. Breeding restricted to Britain, Ireland, northwest France, Scandinavia and northern Russia in east Atlantic. Disperse into coastal waters in winter, young birds migrate to Iberia and northwest Africa. Rare out of sight of land. Young birds have small bills and retain winter plumage in their first summer.

Black Guillemot 35 cm Often called Tystie. Small size; black body except for conspicuous white patch on wing. Bill black and pointed; feet and gape bright red. Winter plumage pale grey, mottled back. Nests in rocky cracks and crevices and also under driftwood, in stone walls and similar sites near beach; sprawling colonies. Breeds on coasts of Britain, Ireland, Iceland and Scandinavia; winters locally. Accidental far from land. Mixed diet of fish, molluscs and invertebrates caught on bottom.

Puffin 30–40 cm Distinctive triangular bill coloured grey, yellow and orange; orange legs. Ornamental orange skin at gape of mouth, over base of bill and above eye shed in winter when bill loses vivid colours. Young birds have shallower, darker coloured bills and greyish faces. Nests in burrows, usually on grassy slopes on cliffs or offshore islands. Breeds in Britain, Ireland, Iceland, northwest France and Norway; disperses to sea after breeding. Regularly seen from land in autumn and spring and offshore in north Atlantic during winter.

Little Auk 24 cm Recognised by small size, stubby bill and white on innermost, tertial, wing feathers which shows in flight and on closed wing. In flight wings beat with fast whirring, body typically dumpy and bill unnoticeable. Feeds on small fish and planktonic crustaceans. Nests in gigantic colonies in boulder scree of cliffs or coastal mountains in High Arctic from Greenland to Siberia. Disperses at sea after breeding avoiding pack ice in winter; rare south to North Sea and accidental off coasts to south or west of this.

Pigeons

Rock Dove 33 cm The only species frequently seen on coast. Grey bird with diagnostic white rump. Nests in caves and crevices of rocky cliffs and explodes from these when disturbed with characteristic clatter of wings. Breeds coastally in western Ireland, northern Scotland, Faeroes, northwest France and also inland

Rock Dove

throughout southern Europe; non-migratory. Beware of confusion with multi-coloured, but sometimes white rumped, racing pigeons which often occur and will even breed on coast. Rock Doves are ancestors of feral pigeons in towns.

In cold weather, **Woodpigeons** may also feed in flocks on saltings and dune slacks when food becomes scarce in their more usual inland habitats.

Passerines

These are mostly small perching birds with unwebbed feet, and many different species occur on the coast as rare or accidental visitors. Those which are common in coastal habitats, either because they breed or feed there in winter, are:
Larks Skylark 17 cm Breeds on saltings and sand dunes, and **Shore**

Shore Lark

Lark 16 cm visits coasts of North Sea in winter from breeding grounds in north and west Scandinavia; both are insect feeders.
Crows Mainly black birds, distinguished by size. **Jackdaw** 32 cm, **Chough** 39 cm, **Carrion Crow** 46 cm and **Raven** 62 cm nest on coastal cliffs and offshore islands, also inland; feed on invertebrates and by scavenging in seabird colonies. Ravens kill birds and small mammals, especially rabbits; Choughs feed only on insects, mainly ants. The sub-species of Carrion Crow breeding in Ireland, northern Scotland, Denmark and Scandinavia is grey-backed and called the Hooded Crow or sometimes the Grey Crow.
Pipits Meadow 15 cm and **Rock** 16 cm are very similar in appearance; both breed and feed, mainly on insects, in coastal habitats. Species separated by song – Meadow Pipit 'parachutes' to ground at end of song flight – and tendency to darker legs in Rock Pipit. Meadow Pipit's pinkish legs can be darkened by mud or seaweed when feeding on shore.
Starling 21 cm Breeds in cliff crevices, often on offshore islands, and flocks on the coast (also inland) in huge numbers during winter. Charac-teristically noisy. Feeds on seeds, insects and other foods from scavenging. Distinct breeding, non-breeding and juvenile plumages.
Finches Commonest species on coast, especially in winter, are **Linnet** 13 cm, **Twite** 13 cm and **Snow Bunting** 16 cm; all are insectivores with sharp, stout bills. First two species feed in flocks, and other species of finch also sometimes flock on coast, especially on saltmarsh, dune slacks or beach tidelines. Cold weather and a scarcity of food inland drives many species to forage outside their normal ranges.

4 What you will see

Some basic advice

Most birds can be recognised with experience by their flight, call, shape, size and more obvious plumage characteristics without binoculars if a good view is obtained. However, as birds are often seen far away and only for long enough to glimpse their appearance, binoculars are invaluable. They are also essential to separate easily confused species such as divers in winter plumage. Birds can be identified at distances of half a kilometre or more using binoculars, and without them seawatching (see page 119) is impossible. Binoculars are also necessary in order to watch birds closely, rather than just identify species. Many fascinating details of a bird's appearance and behaviour, which would otherwise go unnoticed, become visible with a little extra magnification. A telescope is useful for long-distance identification, especially for seawatching, and can also be used for specialised observations such as reading ring numbers or recording the fish brought to chicks (see Chapter 5). At first a pair of binoculars may seem awkward to carry around and difficult to use effectively. With practice, however, finding and focusing on the birds, even flying ones, in the field of vision becomes automatic, and a pair of binoculars soon feels like a second pair of eyes.

Selecting the most suitable pair of binoculars is extremely important as there are many different kinds to choose from. Contrary to uninformed opinion, the largest pair is not always the best. You must begin by deciding what you want from your binoculars and how much you are able to pay. Once again, the most expensive makes are not necessarily the best choice as many kinds of good cheap binoculars are available. Apart from price, binoculars vary most in their size, weight, strength and magnification. Generally, binoculars with low magnification are usually fairly small and therefore light, and tend to be among the cheaper models. These give a less detailed view than those with higher magnification which are larger, sometimes but not always, depending on the make, heavier and can be difficult to hold steady for long periods. Binoculars with very high magnifications of over × 12 are not recommended for beginners as they have to be used with a tripod or rested on a support for a clear view.

Figure 36 Kittiwakes are the only true cliff-nesting gulls, and much of their behaviour has been adapted to the restrictions of space and, for the young, to the avoidance of falling from the nest.

Two numbers are written on the outside of a pair of binoculars; these are the magnification, the number of times the image is magnified, and the lens size, the diameter of the objective (larger) lens in millimetres. A rough estimate of how much light the binoculars let in and hence how suitable they are for viewing in low light intensities like dawn or dusk, can be calculated by dividing the lens size, the second figure, by the magnification, the first figure. The binoculars commonly available and suitable for use in coastal habitats are of the following sizes: 8 × 30, 8 × 40, 9 × 40 and 10 × 50. The second and fourth of these, both with an index of 5, will be the best for viewing in low light conditions although the first, with an index of 3.75, will probably be the smallest and lightest to carry around. The field of view of the binoculars, or how much you can see at a time, is related to the binoculars' magnification (see figure 38), and must also be considered when a choice is being made.

Figure 38 A comparison of the same view through two pairs of binoculars shows how 10 × 50 binoculars give greater magnification but a smaller field of view.

Binoculars are essential for birdwatching, but a telescope is regarded as an optional extra although very handy on the coast. The main advantage of a telescope over binoculars is the greater magnification, but it is also heavy and an extra object to carry around. Telescopes must almost always be used with some kind of a support, usually a tripod, especially when in use at high magnifications. Most telescopes and also a few makes of binoculars will 'zoom' from low magnification (usually about × 15) to high (× 60 or above) which is a great advantage for birdwatching. As with binoculars there are many kinds of telescopes available, some at relatively low prices. Again care must be taken to choose the make that best suits your needs.

Figure 37 The cliffs of Noss, one of the Shetland Isles, rise to 150 metres and provide a home for many thousands of nesting seabirds. The Gannets are most easily visible, and the strand of brown dots low down on the cliff are Guillemots. A colony like this provides insurmountable problems for population censuses!

Consult an experienced birdwatcher when selecting binoculars or a telescope and, if possible, visit several different shops with the same person to compare makes and prices. No assistant should mind you looking through the binoculars and telescopes for sale in the shop. The British Trust for Ornithology publishes a useful guide *Binoculars, Telescopes and Cameras for the Birdwatcher* by J. J. M. Flegg which should also be read before deciding on a purchase.

A notebook and pencil (biros tend to dry up completely or leak copiously) are also useful when birdwatching on the coast. Records of where you go, what you see and the number of birds of each kind present on a particular day are useful for planning a birdwatching trip in the future, and can sometimes be contributed to a local or national study (see Chapter 5). If you are unsure of a bird's identification, a quick sketch or notes on its plumage and behaviour will be a help when looking it up in a guide later. Should you find a rare bird, usually one that is far outside its normal range, it is particularly important to be able to write an accurate description of its appearance so that the record can be officially reported and accepted; notes taken soon after the bird is seen are useful for this. Most books on bird identification give an indication of how rarely or frequently each species is seen within the area it covers. The British Trust for Ornithology (see Appendix II), publishes a checklist of British and European birds. If you think you have seen a rare species, you should report it to your local bird club or naturalists' society or to the Rarities Committee of *British Birds* magazine (see Appendix II), through whom all records are officially accepted or rejected. Coastal habitats are exactly the kind of places where rare species often turn up during spring and autumn.

It is almost always possible to find and watch birds whenever you visit the coast but, by choosing the locality and timing of your birdwatching trips, you will ensure you see more birds and of a greater variety. For example, a breeding colony is deserted and silent outside the nesting season and mudflats are covered with water at high tide. In these cases you should select the time of year or the time of day which is best for seeing the birds. Similarly, it is useless visiting an estuary in the hope of seeing seabirds; you must choose the habitat according to the birds you want to see. Your own experience, or that of a fellow birdwatcher, is useful in deciding when and where to go. You may also need up-to-date Ordnance Survey maps of the area you plan to visit; these will show rocky and sandy beaches, sand dune systems, estuaries, cliffs and islands.

Warm clothing and, in most months, waterproof footwear are essential for birdwatching. The coast is always windy and often cold. Watching birds involves long periods of standing, sitting and even lying down. A hide is useful if you plan to watch one group of birds for a long time, especially if you are studying or photographing them. A hide not only acts as a wind break but also allows you to remain fairly close to the birds without disturbing them. Several kinds designed for birdwatching are available and they are widely advertised in the bird magazines listed in Appendix II.

Personal safety

The following points are absolutely essential for you to remember when you are on the coast – both for your own safety and that of the birds.

Avoid being caught by the incoming tide on mudflats or saltmarsh. Check the time of the next high tide before you set out or carry an up-to-date tide table with you. These areas are flat and the tide can come in very fast indeed.

Never try to climb cliffs or steep banks on the coast; one small mistake may be fatal. This is a special risk on offshore islands where communication with the mainland is difficult. Moreover, in such situations accidents often seem to happen when the weather is too rough for rescue boats to put to sea.

Footwear, preferably boots, should have good soles which give plenty of grip when birdwatching near cliffs or steep slopes. Be especially careful during or after wet weather.

Do not disturb any birds anywhere at any time unless it is unavoidable. This is the golden rule of birdwatching and it is often broken either deliberately or through ignorance. All species of nesting birds are at particular risk, and in Britain certain species require a government licence before you can visit their nests. All British birds and their eggs are protected by law, with the exception of a handful of pest species, and similar laws operate in most other European countries.

When birdwatching on reserves or similar areas managed for visitors, always obey notices or the warden's instructions. These are provided to prevent disturbances to the birds and for your own safety.

The birds on a sandy beach

Usual species Wader and gull roosts at high tide, small flocks of feeding waders and gulls. Flocks of passerines, especially in winter. Breeding Little Terns, Ringed Plovers, Oystercatchers and Skylarks. **Occasional species** Injured, sick or oiled seabirds (see Chapter 5), various species of passerines, waders, skuas and terns on migration. **Best times** Roosts well attended in winter, November to February, and in migration season, late July to October and March to May. Breeding season mainly April to early July. Waders and gulls feed at low tide and several hours either side of it, on intertidal sandflats below beach.

Probably the most obvious birds to see on a sandy beach and in most other coastal habitats are the gulls which feed and roost there. Herring Gulls scavenge along the high tideline and patrol holiday beaches for abandoned scraps of food and rubbish. Most species of gulls, but especially Herring and Black-headed Gulls, will feed in shallow pools left behind by the tide, picking out invertebrates and sometimes trampling on one spot to bring food to the surface. Herring Gulls, and occasionally other species, open shellfish they have pecked off the rocks or collected from the sand by flying up into the air and dropping the shell onto the ground to smash it. Unfortunately they cannot distinguish inedible or

Figure 39 Gulls and an Oystercatcher rest and preen on a sandy beach. Most of these are adult Herring Gulls, with the smudged heads typical of wintering birds, but there is a darker first-winter bird preening in the centre and a Lesser Black-backed Gull standing in the waves.

unbreakable objects and sometimes try to smash old light bulbs! Gulls often roost on a sandy beach especially on remote points or undisturbed stretches. They gather into conspicuous flocks often of a hundred or more birds. It is always worth looking carefully through a roosting flock before approaching it as you may be able to pick out birds in immature plumage, or some of the less common species such as Glaucous, Iceland or Little Gulls. Many of the Herring, Common and Black-headed Gulls breeding in north and central Europe winter inland or on the coasts of countries bordering the Atlantic. Flocks increase noticeably in size during winter.

Waders are often found on sandy beaches, usually scattered in small groups along the sand or feeding on sandbanks and flats exposed at low tide. Turnstones and Sanderling are the commonest species and they both feed mainly at the tide's edge. Sanderling are especially easy to identify as they run up and down the beach following the waves. Ringed

Plovers and Turnstones peck amongst the tide wrack left at the top of the beach; this shelters various invertebrates and especially burrowing sandhoppers and insects. Ringed Plovers also forage by running forwards a few steps, then pausing to stand upright for a second or two apparently to locate their prey by sight and sound, then rushing to grab it from the surface of the sand. Turnstones will flick over pebbles or small stones with their bills to find food underneath. Isolated parts of a sandy beach are sometimes used by waders, mainly Oystercatchers, Ringed Plovers, Turnstones, Dunlin and occasionally Grey Plovers, for high tide roosts.

Ringed Plovers and Oystercatchers commonly breed on sandy beaches. Both lay two to four eggs in a shallow nest scrape on the ground, usually on or above the spring high tideline. Nests are difficult to find as they and the eggs are well camouflaged. Oystercatchers start to lay as early as March and Ringed Plovers usually about April or May. In both a territory around the nest is defended from other birds of the same species. The defence is mainly carried out by means of displays of aggression or intended attack made to intruders. The Ringed Plover, like many small waders, may also try to lure a potential predator away from its nest or chicks. The adult bird calls and conspicuously trails one wing, so called injury-feigning, or it may run away silently with a peculiar scuttling motion called rodent-running. Both these displays are meant to attract the predator's attention and lead it away from the nest or young. Oystercatchers walk up and down side by side with their bills pointing stiffly downwards, uttering a short piercing call during disputes over territory.

Figure 40 The Oystercatcher's territorial display is accompanied by repetitive and shrill calls which are so much a part of birdwatching on a sandy beach and elsewhere on the coast in spring. Like most other coastal birds apart from ducks, the male and female Oystercatchers look alike; the two birds here are probably a pair.

Sometimes four or more birds will fly round in circles above their nesting area calling loudly. Chases occur from time to time but you will rarely see an outright fight between birds as the displays of territorial ownership are designed to prevent this.

Ringed Plover and Oystercatcher chicks are almost perfectly camouflaged on hatching, and leave the nest within twenty-four hours. They follow the adults around and peck at everything they find until they gradually learn to feed themselves. When the parents give an alarm call at the approach of a predator or a human the chicks crouch so that they are rarely seen, even on an open beach with little cover. On some beach nature reserves, such as Thornham in Norfolk, managed by the RSPB, hides are situated overlooking areas where Ringed Plovers, Oystercatchers and other species breed, and the chicks can be watched, without disturbance, while they run around the sands. As soon as they are able to fly and feed themselves in about July, the juvenile birds gather into flocks on beaches or estuaries near the breeding grounds where they feed before migrating south for the winter.

Terns can be seen on sandy beaches, usually resting in flocks either after their breeding season between July and August or earlier in May and June if there is a colony nearby. Juvenile birds remain with their parents after leaving the colony and are easily distinguished by their white foreheads. The adults continue to feed their young for several weeks after fledging, and this too sometimes takes place on the beach.

Figure 41 Common Terns at their nest scrape on a sandy beach. The chicks are about a day or two old and already mobile; one camouflaged egg remains still unhatched.

Terns often feed in the shallows just off a sandy beach, drawing attention to themselves by their loud calls to one another as they plunge-dive for fish. If conditions are right for insects to swarm, usually in the evening, terns will sometimes hawk in huge circles high above the beach.

The Little Tern does not breed in dense colonies like other terns, but prefers to nest on sand or shingle with widely spaced nesting territories scattered along a suitable beach at about the level of the spring high tide. Unfortunately, the terns need the same kind of habitat for nesting as a large proportion of the human population needs for sunbathing and other similar activities, and they are often disturbed when nesting. Despite the birds' vociferous defence of their nesting territories and their dive-bombing flights at intruders, many people walk through nesting areas, repeatedly disturbing the birds and even unconsciously trampling nests and eggs. Local wardens in many areas of Britain, particularly in the southeast where most Little Terns nest, and other countries have successfully reduced unintentional disturbance by erecting wire fences and appropriate notices around tern breeding areas on more popular beaches. Often the birds which nest on unprotected parts of the beach and lose clutches early in the season, move to wardened areas to lay again, so that nesting densities are exceptionally high on some beach reserves. At one site in the south of England, over 200 pairs of Little Terns nest together. Such large concentrations of tern nests attract predators, particularly ground predators like foxes, stoats, cats and mink (both wild animals and escapes from fur farms). The main reason that Little Terns usually nest at low densities is to avoid the attentions of predators like these but, when disturbance forces the birds into almost colonial situations, losses of eggs and young and even the breeding birds themselves can be severe. This species like all the terns is particularly interesting to watch at the nest with its noisy feeding of chicks and courtship presentation of fish, but great care must be taken to avoid disturbance.

Another seabird which can be found breeding on sandy shores is the Black Guillemot; this species also breeds on rocky shores and low cliffs where it is slightly more common. Nests are hidden under driftwood or in holes and crevices in low sand banks often found at the top of the beach, or even in cavities of nearby stone walls. The birds lay two eggs – unlike the other auks which lay only one – in about May, and can be watched bringing fish and various marine invertebrates back to the nest when the chicks hatch in June. The high-pitched squeaky calls of the adults make nests fairly easy to find. Individual birds sometimes have a preference for certain types of food so that you may notice, for example, that one bird will bring the chicks a single large fish at each meal, whilst its mate arrives with loads of tiny crustaceans. Like other auks, Black Guillemots carry the food whole in the bill which makes it possible to record exactly what the chicks are fed. The young remain with their parents after fledging in July, and family groups are often seen on the water in breeding areas. The birds dive from the surface and swim underwater to catch fish; if timed, it is surprising to see how long they stay submerged.

Other birds to look for on a sandy beach are Cormorants and Shags which often sit out on groynes and breakwaters with their wings spread (see page 32). These two species and divers, grebes, Eider and other diving duck, which also swim underwater to collect food from the bottom, sometimes forage close in to the beach at high tide. The rubbish and vegetation on the upper part of the beach shelters insects and other invertebrates which attract flocks of Starlings, finches, Snow Buntings, larks and various crows in winter.

The birds in sand dunes

Usual species Nesting gulls, terns, Shelduck, Eiders, Skylarks and pipits. In winter, wildfowl and flocks of passerines. **Occasional species** Birds of prey, Whooper Swans, various migrant passerines seeking shelter. Nesting Fulmars. **Best times** In winter months, November to March, dunes provide alternative feeding for many passerines and both shelter and food for wildfowl. In summer the nesting season lasts from about April to July.

The coast is usually very windy and sand dunes provide shelter for birds. Exhausted migrants, making a first landfall after a sea crossing, often stop to feed and rest in dunes. For this reason it is worth checking the identification of all small birds seen here during the autumn. In coastal areas where dunes develop naturally without reclamation or alteration by Man, they can occupy large areas some distance from the sea. Some parts of the dunes are sufficiently remote from human disturbance and ground predators to make suitable nesting sites for gulls, terns and duck.

The two species of duck most commonly found nesting in sand dunes are the Shelduck and Eider; both also nest on small offshore islands. Other ducks including Pintail will also nest in dunes. Flocks of Eider gather in sheltered water near the dunes such as an estuary in April or May, and paired birds feed on the beach nearby during courtship. The drakes defend the ducks from the attentions of intruding males, so that they can spend as much time as possible feeding. This is important because the ducks lay eggs and incubate for three to four weeks without feeding again. In pairs which breed successfully, usually the older, more experienced birds, the drake's protection allows the duck to build up enough reserves for a clutch of four or five eggs. Younger drakes, breeding later in the season, are less attentive to their mates during courtship and their ducks are able to lay only two or three eggs. Nest sites, selected by the females in dune slacks or adjacent moorland, are well covered by vegetation and camouflaged from predators. Flocks of drakes, with only a few ducks among them, are a common feature of estuaries and seas near sand dunes where Eiders are breeding. The ducks incubate the eggs un-

Figure 42 A furtive Shelduck prospects in the dunes for a nest site under vegetation or in a disused burrow.

aided by the drakes, and bring the young ducklings to the sea in a sheltered place a few days after they hatch.

Feeding during courtship is also an important feature of the Shelduck's breeding behaviour. Paired birds can be seen in April or May defending feeding territories on the beach near the dunes where they will nest. The female incubates a clutch of eight to ten eggs laid in a hole or deep under vegetation for about a month, attended by the drake. The ducklings are accompanied to the water by both adults soon after hatching in June. Family groups and crèches, where many ducklings are guarded by a few adults, will also be seen at about this time.

Other ducks use the pools and marshes in dune slacks for shelter and feeding during winter. Flocks of Mallard, Teal and Wigeon are the commonest species. The first two species feed in the water by up-ending or dabbling, depending on its depth, and Teal also pick seeds and other food items from amongst the half-submerged vegetation. Wigeon feed mainly on land, grazing grass. Whooper Swans also occasionally feed during migration or in winter by grazing on the flatter, wetter areas of the dune system, usually furthest inland. Both these areas and the damper slacks are feeding and roosting grounds for gulls (chiefly Herring and Great Black-backed Gulls), Lapwings and sometimes Golden Plovers. Their food is collected by picking small items from the ground surface; the prey consists mainly of various invertebrates.

Gulls and terns nest in slacks in the remoter parts of the dunes in some

Figure 43 A difference of opinion over territorial boundaries by nesting Lesser Black-backed Gulls in the dunes. Displays of aggression – seen here as grass pulling – usually take the place of outright fights. Grass pulling is a displacement activity and can be compared with the angry man who hits the table instead of his enemy.

areas. The colonies are reoccupied in March and April, and the usual species are Herring and Lesser Black-backed Gulls with some Great Black-backed Gulls. Courtship and pairing takes place and nesting territories are established by a system of displays and calls used as signals or warnings to other birds. From now until the colony is deserted at the end of the breeding season in August the area is never quiet; even during the night a few gulls can be heard calling and a great din fills the daylight hours.

A clutch of usually three speckled eggs are laid by each pair and incubated in turn by both birds for about one month. Off duty birds spend most of their time preening, defending the nesting territory against their neighbours or feeding away from the colony. Incubating birds sit motionless but rise every half hour or so to turn the eggs. When the young hatch in June, they are fed on the territory by both adults on regurgitated, partly digested food. They peck at the parent's bill, aiming for the red patch at the tip, to stimulate regurgitation. They grow fast and within a couple of weeks of hatching have changed from inevitably charming, fluffy chicks into gawky, long-legged, pot-bellied young gulls. They are often rather bedraggled around the head from their near-liquid diet and the aggressive pecks they receive from other chicks, or from adult gulls if they stray far from the nest site. At the alarm call of the adults the chicks run for shelter and freeze; their speckled plumage helps to hide them. If the colony is thoroughly disturbed, by a human or a fight between adults for example, chicks scatter in all directions and afterwards risk savage attacks by the adults as they make their way back through other nesting territories to their own. Some chicks are killed in this way and others die from cold, especially in wet weather, or from starvation if they are too small or weak to compete with other chicks for food.

In July, about four weeks after hatching, the young gulls start learning to fly by flapping their wings and jumping up and down. Gradually they acquire the skills of flight and leave the territories; the colony is dotted with grey-backed adults and brown juveniles at this stage. Soon the colony is used only by birds preening and resting. Great Black-backed Gulls occasionally nest singly or in small groups in the dunes. They are voracious predators of other birds' eggs and young and will also kill and eat adult birds.

Common, Arctic, Sandwich and, sometimes, rare Roseate Terns will all breed in sand dunes. Nesting terns are a fascinating sight but a hide is essential for watching them if disturbance is to be avoided. Many coastal reserves have hides where this is possible (see page 72), and the use of these is strongly recommended. Terns return to the colony later in the spring than gulls because they have further to travel from their winter quarters off west Africa. The first to arrive are usually Sandwich Terns,

Figure 44 Sandwich Terns nesting at typically high density at De Beer on the Dutch coast. Some birds have the characteristic head crests raised; note also the very short legs visible in the standing birds.

followed a few weeks later by Common and Arctic Terns, and finally by Roseates which winter the furthest south.

Courtship involves the feeding of the female by the male bird and many other displays by the birds both on the ground and in flight. Nesting territories are established and defended from other birds, and a two or three egg clutch is laid during June in a shallow scrape on the ground which serves as a nest. Sandwich Terns pack their nests closely together so that sitting birds are only just out of range of their neighbours' bills. They prefer open areas of the colony with short grass, whilst Common and Arctic Terns are more scattered with lower nest densities, and Roseate Terns often hide their nests under plants or even in disused rabbit burrows. The eggs are well camouflaged and the birds fly off the nest and mob any potential predator or human approaching the colony. Both birds of a pair share incubation and fish is sometimes brought to the incubating bird when its mate arrives to relieve it.

When the chicks hatch they are well camouflaged by their speckled plumage and leave the scrape almost immediately to shelter under vegetation nearby. The adults bring whole fish, usually sandeels, to feed the chicks and call them from hiding. Sandwich Tern chicks join a crèche in the colony a few days after hatching, and both adults are able to collect food for them. The chicks recognise their own parents by their calls when they return to the crèche with fish. The young terns have learnt to fly by late June but continue to be fed by their parents for a month or more after fledging. The family groups usually disperse locally at this stage before migrating southwards in autumn. Colour ringing has proved that juveniles are still occasionally fed by their parents when they reach west Africa in November.

Concentrations of nesting terns in dunes near the coast and elsewhere

Figure 45 A 'dread' or mass flight from the colony by Arctic Terns. This display is usually caused by disturbance and is preceded by a sudden silence in the colony.

sometimes attract Arctic Skuas passing on migration. The skuas specialise in chasing birds to steal their food and the hundreds of terns carrying fish to a breeding colony provide the skuas with plenty of opportunities. There can be few more exciting episodes to watch than an Arctic Skua chasing a tern as they are well matched in speed and agility of flight.

Figure 46 A dark plumage phase Arctic Skua chases a Common Tern carrying fish. The tern will be harried until it drops its fish which will then be retrieved by the skua before it reaches the ground.

The Fulmar is another bird sometimes found breeding on sand dunes although it is more usually found on cliff ledges. On the Sands of Forvie, northeast Scotland, for example, Fulmars lay on sandy ledges in the steeper dunes near the sea, especially in sites protected by overhanging tussocks of vegetation. The breeding behaviour of the Fulmar is described on page 103.

Other nesting birds to watch out for are Skylarks and Meadow Pipits. Both make song flights and are easily recognised when singing. Like other small passerines the cock feeds the hen during courtship. This behaviour, the repeated territorial singing and the birds carrying nesting material or food for chicks are sure indications of breeding areas. Sometimes many patient hours of watching are needed before the nest of either species can be found and care must be taken not to keep birds off the nest too long. Chicks are often seen being fed by the adults once they have left the nest from late May onwards.

Finches and Starlings feed in dunes during autumn and winter. These can also be interesting to watch as each flock of Starlings has its own hierarchy so that certain individuals can always displace others from food without dispute. Carrion Crows, often in family groups after the breeding season, and Jackdaw flocks occur in dunes, and can be seen strutting about scavenging for food. Kestrels also hunt in dunes, catching small birds and mammals and large insects. Other birds of prey to look out for are both Hen and Marsh Harriers and Short-eared Owls.

The birds on mudflats

Common species At low tide nearly all waders, Grey Heron, geese, ducks and gulls. Also Cormorants, divers and grebes at high tide. **Occasional species** Accidental visitors. Some waders are more common than others. **Best times** Migration from late July to October, and March to early May and winter seasons. Low tide and several hours either side of it for birds feeding on mud.

Mudflats are a rich feeding habitat for coastal birds, whether they are situated in an estuary, isolated on a sheltered stretch of coast or in an urban area. Most mudflats are, by definition, intertidal and therefore almost completely covered by water at high tide. For all but the aquatic birds feeding is impossible at high tide and a few hours either side of it – the exact period depends on the topography of the mudflat. The birds move away to a high tide roost, often on a nearby remote sandy beach or shingle spit where they can watch for any predators that may approach.

Waders are the most numerous and obvious birds on a mudflat at low tide. They spread over a wide area, feeding singly, in groups or in close

Figure 47 A flock of waders gathering to roost on the Dee estuary as the incoming tide pushes them off their feeding grounds. Waders are usually counted at high tide because at other times they are spread out over a huge area of mudflats.

flocks, their distribution reflecting the availability of their food. It is possible to predict roughly where each species will be found by knowing the basic diet and feeding methods of each species and by noting the types of food present on different parts of the mudflats as indicated by mussel beds, worm casts and so on. Most birds use several feeding techniques in quick succession. Long-billed waders tend to probe into the mud for food, and short-billed species like the Turnstone pick items from the surface by stabbing with their bills, or poking among stones. Godwits, Oystercatchers, Redshanks, Spotted Redshanks, Greenshanks, Curlews and usually Dunlin all take worms and other burrowing invertebrates from the mud (see figure 19). Extraction of food is sometimes difficult and the bird will walk round in a circle with its bill in the mud, straining in different directions. Large food items can be seen in the bill before being swallowed but in small birds like the Dunlin, the food is rarely visible.

A wader's bill length determines how far down it can probe for food and also the depth of water in which it can feed. The bill lengths of the male and female Bar-tailed Godwit differ by anything up to thirty per cent; males have bills measuring less than 86 mm while those of the females are always more than 87 mm. When they feed at the tide edge, as they often do, females can take food from significantly deeper water than males. It has been argued that this helps them avoid competing for their favourite food of burrowing worms, particularly the lugworm, especially during cold weather when food is scarce because the worms go deep into the mud. Beware of trying to identify waders probing in thick mud by bill colour for their bills will often be muddy. The small-billed waders, like Ringed Plovers, stints, Lapwings, Grey and Golden Plovers, feed by walking and running over the mud to grab food from the surface.

Some idea of waders' diets can be obtained by watching them feeding and also by the careful examination of regurgitated pellets containing indigestible food remains. These are very delicate and break up into a heap of shell and other fragments as soon as they reach the mud. Pellets can be collected from all parts of the mudflats where waders rest whilst feeding; such areas are marked by many white droppings and also, in the autumn, by moulted feathers. Some pellets can be found at high tide roosts. The actual identification of food species in the pellets is difficult and requires examination under a microscope although shell fragments are usually fairly obvious. Worms and other soft-bodied prey are poorly represented in the pellets but can sometimes be identified under a microscope by the bristles from their bodies.

Note the different plumages of waders on a mudflat. In spring many of the birds progress quite far into summer plumage before leaving western Europe for their nesting grounds, and this gives some idea of their splendid appearance whilst breeding. In the autumn, juvenile birds of most species can be distinguished by their less worn feathers and speckled colours. Young Oystercatchers have dull brown bills and dark eyes, and lack the white collar of the adults in their first winter of life. Adult waders begin their wing moult in the autumn, often while making use of the rich food supply on coastal mudflats. In the larger species, like the Curlew and Oystercatcher, the missing feathers and new ones growing into the gaps on the wing are easily visible when the birds fly overhead. A Sanderling in wing moult is shown in figure 25.

Wader roosts can be a spectacular sight, mainly because of the sheer numbers of birds involved. No idea of how many birds use a mudflat can be gained by watching them at low tide as they are widely scattered and some birds are hidden in channels. As the tide slithers in across the flats however, the birds are gradually pushed back towards the shore. Sometimes the first sign of this to a birdwatcher on the sea wall overlooking the mudflat is the increasing noise of wader calls. Most waders can swim if necessary but prefer to roost on dry land or in shallow water. Flocks gather on isolated points and spits uncovered by water and gradually merge and retreat until a single large roost forms on an unsubmerged site. The birds preen, rest and sleep in the roost. Numbers are sometimes enormous. Reports of roosting flocks on a favourite wader estuary in the French Vendée during autumn describe how the smallest Dunlin have to stand underneath the Redshanks, and these under the Curlews and godwits in order to save space! A flock of waders on the move is always fascinating. The birds are perfectly coordinated with each other as they twist and turn in flight. Often when coming in to land they sweep over and back before alighting which creates a unique sight and has to be seen to be appreciated.

Other birds beside waders which are regularly seen on a mudflat are ducks and geese. The dabbling ducks – Shovelers, Wigeon, Mallard, Teal and Pintails – feed in shallow water over the mud by pecking or sieving food from the surface, or collecting it by dipping the head underwater or by up-ending. They also sometimes submerge completely. Only Shelduck and Wigeon habitually feed out on the mud itself, though Teal and Mallard do so occasionally. Shelduck can be seen digging or using a scything action with their spoon-like bills when feeding in wet mud, to sieve out minute food items; they also trample the mud to bring food to the surface. Molluscs and crustaceans, particularly the marine snail *Hydrobia*, are their main food. Wigeon are vegetarians and usually feed on land but on mudflats they graze on sea lettuce and the slimy green seaweed *Enteromorpha*. Teal and Mallard use their bills to filter food from the mud. Brent Geese prefer mudflats to all other coastal habitats in winter. They are the only geese to be dependent on intertidal feeding for their over-winter survival. Like Wigeon, they are vegetarians and graze on eel grass or, when supplies of this are exhausted late in winter,

Figure 48 Cormorants (below) and Shags build large untidy nests and usually rear three young. Like the Cormorant, the Shag (above) has bare skin on its throat but grows a crest during the breeding season. The brilliant eye and the beautiful green sheen and scalloping on the feathers are visible in both species at close range.

Figure 50 Dark-bellied Brent Geese on a mudflat, grazing on seaweed exposed at low tide. Nearly a quarter of the total northwest European wintering population of this subspecies occurs on the Essex coast.

on *Enteromorpha*. The family groups of Brent Geese remain together during winter so that the proportion of young birds in a flock, recognised by the lack of white markings on the neck and barring on closed wing, gives an indication of the nesting success in the Arctic the previous summer.

Other birds feeding on intertidal mudflats are the gulls, mainly Herring, Lesser Black-backed, Great Black-backed, Common and Black-headed. These collect invertebrates from the mud's surface, especially molluscs such as mussels, cockles and whelks, crustaceans such as crabs and shrimps and echinoderms such as starfish. Herring Gulls can smash open bivalve shells by flying up and dropping the shell onto hard ground. Common and Black-headed Gulls have the habit of trampling in one spot in shallow water to bring small food items out of the mud and up to the surface. The Grey Heron visits pools and creeks on the mudflat to stalk stranded fish, eels or exposed invertebrates left behind by the tide. Carrion Crows and Jackdaws also sometimes scavenge on mudflats, and the former will open shells by dropping them like a gull. When the tide turns and water covers the mud, vast amounts of food are made available to any birds which can swim and dive, especially since most of the mud-dwelling invertebrates are active only when underwater. Many of the ducks continue feeding, by head-dipping or up-

Figure 49 A Fulmar uses an updraft to glide past a clifftop. The straight wings are held stiff and the tail is spread and angled to guide the bird.

Figure 51 An adult Black-headed Gull in winter plumage feeds in an intertidal pool by trampling in one spot to stir up invertebrates buried in the mud.

ending, in the water covering the mud. Diving ducks such as Eider, Scaup, Goldeneye and Long-tailed Ducks move into the area in flocks, with Cormorants, grebes and divers. Extensive mudflats form only on sheltered shores, especially in estuaries, and such areas are ideal wintering grounds for these species. The main foods they take are bottom-living molluscs and crustaceans and some echinoderms. Diving duck usually submerge for about half a minute and feed in water two to five metres deep, but Long-tailed Duck often reach depths of ten metres.

The birds on a saltmarsh

Common species Most waders and dabbling ducks, some more common than others. Gulls, finch flocks, Starlings and other passerines. **Occasional species** Accidental visitors. **Best times** Migration season from late July to October and March to early May for waders. Winter months for both ducks and waders. Summer months for a few of the breeding species. Low tide for feeding birds, high tide for roosts.

Saltmarsh provides a variety of feeding habitats for birds, mainly divided between the muddy channels and pools, and the vegetated higher parts of the marsh. Most of the saltmarsh is covered with water or waterlogged at high tide, although the area under water depends on the height of each tide. Birds feeding on the marsh which prefer not to swim (mainly waders) gather into high tide roosts on the innermost, higher areas or, on high spring tides, on inland fields.

Waders are common and numerous on saltmarsh and most of the species which are found on mudflats also occur on the muddy parts of a saltmarsh. The species which particularly prefer drainage channels and marsh feeding to open flats are the Greenshank, Green, Common and Wood Sandpipers, Ruff, stints and Snipe. The other common birds are Curlew, Dunlin, Redshank and Spotted Redshank. Most of the food is collected by probing and pecking in the mud under the vegetation. As the circulation of water at high tide is slowed down by the presence of plants, a large range of different invertebrates find shelter and suitable homes in and on saltmarsh mud. Insects living among the plants on the driest pieces of marsh also provide food for waders. Birds are often secretive on saltmarsh, hiding in the vegetation and deep in drainage channels but with careful stalking they can be approached close enough to watch them feeding.

Redshanks and, in some northern areas, Dunlin nest on saltmarsh. The birds take up breeding territories in May and these are advertised and defended by song, either in flight by Dunlin or from a suitable perch by Redshanks. The nests are well hidden and blend in with the ground

Figure 52 A typical Redshank perch on the nesting territory. Display flights and loud calls are used to advertise ownership and intruders or potential predators are mobbed and driven away.

vegetation; usually three or four eggs are laid. The young hatch out in June and follow their parents around almost immediately, feeding and being fed on insects and larvae collected from the surrounding plants. A very high tide during the breeding season can be disastrous as it washes away nests and young chicks. Usually nesting is timed to coincide with low neap tides but stormy weather can cause the tide to cover the saltmarsh unexpectedly.

Ducks are the other common inhabitants of a saltmarsh. Mallard, Shelduck and Eider sometimes take their ducklings there from nearby nesting grounds, but most ducks use saltmarsh for winter feeding only.

Figure 53 Shelducks feed in the shallow water of a saltmarsh drainage channel by dabbling on the surface and up-ending to collect small invertebrates, sieving them out of the water with their bills. Unlike waders, Shelducks can feed at all stages of the tide if necessary.

The Shelduck and the dabbling ducks are the commonest species. Shelduck feed in wet mud and take insects from the vegetation. The other species specialise in collecting seeds from saltmarsh plants and also catch insects. The main seeding plants are orache on the upper parts of the marsh, and glasswort. The former are especially preferred by Mallard. Teal rely mainly on seeds for their winter diet and their small bills are adapted for picking up food of this kind; they often feed by night and, like other ducks and waders, make best use of all low tide hours for foraging on saltmarsh.

Other birds you may see on a saltmarsh are the Grey Heron, foraging stealthily around muddy pools and streams, numerous gulls especially Herring and Black-headed, Carrion Crows and Jackdaws, and flocks of finches, larks and pipits collecting insects and seeds. Black-headed Gulls sometimes nest on saltmarsh, although they are rarely successful in rearing young because high tides often cover the marshes where they are breeding and wash away the nests and young. Their breeding season lasts from about May to July.

The birds on a shingle beach

Common species Gulls, Turnstones and Oystercatchers. High tide roosts of waders and gulls. **Occasional species** Other waders. **Best times** None; roosts are largest in autumn and winter from late August to March. Tides have little effect on this habitat.

Shingle beaches are comparatively poor places for birds to feed as the constant wash of waves and long-shore drift combine to make most shingle unsuitable for invertebrates. However, Turnstones can sometimes be seen flicking over pebbles to collect food and Oystercatchers manage to extract lugworms from shingle in sheltered areas. Some other waders including Dunlin, Sanderlings and Ringed Plovers stop briefly on migration to feed. Ringed Plovers and Oystercatchers nest on broad shingle beaches and remote spits just as they do on sandy beaches. Little Terns also prefer shingle, especially spits, to nest on although high tides and disturbance by humans, especially fishermen, cause problems. For example, a total of over 200 pairs of Little Terns have been recorded

Figure 54 An Oystercatcher settles onto its eggs amongst the shingle. The breast feathers are puffed up to allow the eggs to come into contact with the brood patch, a bare piece of skin heavily supplied with blood vessels.

Figure 55 Ringed Plovers at their nest scrape on shingle. The male bird (left) is being relieved by the female who will continue incubation of the four eggs.

nesting along the twenty-two kilometres of shingle on Chesil Beach in southern England.

The opportunistic scavengers, Herring and Great Black-backed Gulls, Jackdaws and Carrion Crows, are also seen on shingle beaches. Groynes, constructed to reduce erosion, are favourite perches for Cormorants and Shags. Finches and insect-feeding passerines are sometimes attracted to the high tide line, especially if it is vegetated.

The birds on a rocky shore

Common species Oystercatchers, Turnstones, Purple Sandpipers, Redshanks, Curlews, diving birds just offshore, gulls, Starlings and Rock Pipits. **Occasional species** Other waders and passerines. Breeding terns and Black Guillemots. **Best times** None; late summer and autumn from July to October are best for waders, and winter for flocks of diving duck and grebes offshore. Low tide period for intertidal feeding.

The Oystercatcher, Turnstone and Purple Sandpiper specialise in feeding on rocky shores. In fact, the latter is rarely seen elsewhere outside the breeding season. The Oystercatcher's bill is designed for removing shell-fish from the rocks and extracting the soft-bodied animals. The bill is stout and strong and used as a lever or cutter. When the bird feeds on bivalve molluscs, like the piddock, mussel, cockle, scallop or razor shell, it inserts the tip of its bill between the two halves of the shell in exactly the right position to cut the strong muscles holding the shell together.

This is done so skilfully that the animal has no time to close the shell tightly and prevent the Oystercatcher's bill entering. Gastropod molluscs, such as whelks, limpets, top shells and periwinkles, are also attacked with speed, and prised from the rock before they can withdraw their 'foot' and close the operculum over the shell's entrance. Some Oystercatchers habitually feed inland, usually on wet fields on the coast where they probe for earthworms and other invertebrates, or on mudflats. Other individuals prefer to feed on rocky shores where they feed mainly on molluscs. On examination of a large number of birds in Britain from both groups, it was found that Oystercatchers feeding on soft substrates had longer, more pointed bills, adapted for probing and grasping, than the rocky shore birds whose bills were blunt and chisel-like for forcing and slicing.

Purple Sandpipers and Turnstones usually occur in large numbers on rocky beaches. High tide roosts during the autumn migration can contain up to several hundred birds in mixed flocks. The birds feed by probing and picking invertebrates from between rocks and stones, and from

Figure 56 The Turnstone, as its name suggests, uses its short, stout bill to flick over stones and peck up invertebrates from underneath. This is a typical sight on a rocky shore.

under pebbles which they overturn. Numbers are deceiving as many birds will be out of sight among the rocks. Both species also scavenge on the high tideline, and there is one often-quoted record of Turnstones feeding on a human corpse. The banks of rotting seaweed stranded by high tides during stormy weather are favourite feeding sites for Purple Sandpipers, Turnstones, Herring, Glaucous and Great Black-backed

Figure 57 A Ruff feeds on flies and grubs in rotting seaweed. Ruffs are commonly found in saltmarsh creeks and at coastal sewage farms but they stop off on migration to take advantage of the rich feeding in banks of stranded seaweed on rocky or sandy shores.

Gulls and other birds. The seaweed is covered with flies and infested with their eggs and later their grubs; the surface layer is usually alive with sandhoppers. The birds take all these foods and can be attracted onto a weed bank if the surface layer is kicked away to expose the grubs beneath. Gulls and, particularly in Iceland, phalaropes also feed on the débris which floats out of the bank as it partly submerges at high tide. Feeding of this kind is a rich source of energy to migrant birds. Consecutive catches of Purple Sandpipers and Turnstones which had been feeding on seaweed banks during the autumn in Iceland showed that the birds could gain up to twelve or fifteen grams in weight per day. Other waders often seen on rocky shores, especially in autumn and spring, are Redshanks, Common Sandpipers and Curlews.

Pools left by the tide attract Grey Herons and sometimes ducks. Wigeon may be found feeding on weeds such as *Enteromorpha* and *Ulva* which grow on intertidal rock surfaces. Passerines, especially Starlings and the ubiquitous crows, also feed at low tide, and rocky beaches are a favourite feeding habitat for Rock Pipits. These and other insectivorous birds will often forage on seaweed banks with the waders.

At high tide there is rich underwater feeding for birds. Diving species including the Cormorant, Shag, grebes, divers, seaduck (especially

Eider), and auks (mainly Black Guillemot), can all be watched feeding close in to the shore over a rocky bottom.

Few birds breed on rocky shores as they are usually too exposed and offer relatively small areas of non-tidal habitat. Shores of low-lying islands are often rocky and sometimes provide sites for Common and Arctic Terns to breed. Ringed Plovers and Oystercatchers occasionally breed on the upper tideline of a rocky shore. Black Guillemots nest where the boulders form a scree on the shoreline.

The birds on cliffs and islands

Common species Cliff-nesting auks, Fulmar, Gannet, Cormorant, Shag, Kittiwake and crows. Island-nesting petrels, skuas, gulls, terns and ducks. Mid-winter roosts of gulls and wildfowl on islands. **Occasional species** Migrants and accidental visitors, especially on islands. **Best times** Seabird breeding seasons roughly March to May for courtship and May to early August for main nesting.

Wherever the shoreline rises into cliffs and the geological strata are suitable, seabirds will almost certainly be found nesting. Mainland cliffs have to be sheer and inaccessible to ground predators before they are colonised by birds but on offshore islands and stacks cliffs are very often occupied. Low-lying islands are used by many ground-nesting species. All the main seabird colonies in northwest Europe are found in the areas bordering the warm northward flowing branch of the Gulf Stream, the North Atlantic Drift (see page 13), where the mixing of currents causes upwelling and rich productivity at sea; this, in turn, provides rich fishing for birds and Man alike as explained in Chapter 1. The birds which feed offshore, at least to the edge of the continental shelf, tend to breed in large colonies, often with high densities of nests. Colonies of seabirds on cliffs often contain as many as ten or more species nesting together and total many thousands of birds.

The auks are probably the most spectacular of all cliff-breeding birds, mainly because of the huge numbers associated with each colony. Breeding seabirds cannot really be imagined until you have seen, smelled and heard a cliff of nesting Guillemots in June or July. Auks are absent from the breeding cliffs in winter although Guillemots, which spend the winter months just offshore, sometimes come to land for a while, often early in the morning, between late November and March. By March, if the weather is reasonable, flocks of Razorbills, Guillemots and Puffins start to gather below the nesting cliffs in huge rafts. Peak numbers can be seen in the mornings. Courtship and pairing takes place on the sea and in Razorbills and Guillemots this is accompanied by communal displays of formation swimming and simultaneous diving, sometimes called 'water games'. Courtship and the selection of nest sites continue when the birds come to land in March and April. Auks are faithful to their mate of the previous season, as far as annual mortality allows, and they usually retain the same nest site. Throughout the breeding season Puffins come to land in large numbers but only late in the afternoon and evening. This is worth remembering if you visit a seabird colony during the day hoping to see Puffins.

The cliff-nesting auks avoid competition for nest sites by different habitat preferences. Guillemots nest in masses on the rock ledges of the cliff, inside shallow caves and on top of pedestal-like rocks and offshore

Figure 58 A cliff colony of seabirds with Guillemots crowding on narrow rock ledges, and Kittiwake nests built onto the rock face. These species can only be counted when they come to land to breed. In this picture there are about 32 sitting Kittiwakes and 136 Guillemots.

stacks. Razorbills use mainly isolated sites, often among the Guillemot ledges, in cracks and crevices, on small ledges, between and underneath boulders and occasionally even in shallow earth burrows. They are quick to take advantage of any new habitat offered, as for example on the seabird island of Skokholm off the coast of south Wales. On one occasion, a cargo of coal from a ship wrecked on the island was piled at the top of one of the cliffs and, before it could be transported, Razorbills had laid eggs in its cavities. Puffins always nest in earth burrows in grass slopes on the cliff, usually at the top on the extreme edge or sometimes among boulders. The nitrogen-rich guano produced by auks and all the other seabirds nesting on an exposed and otherwise salty cliff, causes the growth of thick vegetation including some plant species not recorded elsewhere. The burrowing activity of Puffins like that of Manx Shearwaters and rabbits can cause the development of a distinctive vegetation often dominated by sorrel or orache.

With the exception of the Black Guillemot, all auks lay a single egg without building a nest. Laying takes place in May and June and if the first egg is lost early in incubation it may be replaced by another. Losses are due mainly to predation by Herring and Great Black-backed Gulls, Jackdaws and sometimes skuas, or to desertion or infertility. Incubation is shared by both the birds in a pair for about thirty-five days. The Guillemots and Razorbills, which can often be watched nesting in quite open sites, spend minutes on end preening each other, touching bills and

Figure 59 A Puffin colony can often be recognised by the burrow-riddled turf. Many burrows cave in and become overgrown; the birds can dig themselves new ones although they prefer to take over a rabbit or Manx Shearwater burrow if possible.

calling in displays which strengthen the pair bond. When the chick hatches, it is covered with down but well developed. It grows quickly, fed on fish (mainly sprats in the Guillemot and sandeels in the Razorbill) which are brought whole in the adult's bill. When less than three weeks old, only about one-third adult size, and still unable to fly, the chick leaves the nest site and goes down to the sea with one of the parents. This is called 'fledging' although the chick can only glide down to the water on stubby undeveloped wings and it takes place in the evening twilight in order to reduce the chance of predation by gulls. The vital link between parent and young is maintained by frantic calling. If all goes well the two birds swim out to sea and do not return to land again until the next summer in the case of the adult, or two or more years later in the case of the juvenile. The fledging of Razorbills and Guillemots is one of the most extraordinary sights in the seabird world, as anyone who has witnessed it will agree.

Figure 60 Like all auks, the Puffin shown here and Razorbill (figure 61) are adapted for underwater swimming rather than aerial agility. Their wings are short and beat fast in flight, and both the tail and feet are needed to manoeuvre the birds in mid-air. They bring whole fish to their chicks but largely avoid competition for food during the breeding season; the Puffin tends to collect many small sandeels and the Razorbill fewer, large ones.

Puffins continue to feed their chicks in the burrow for about five weeks after hatching. Then the young bird, more than half grown and well able to fly, goes off to sea on its own under the protective cover of darkness. Auks rarely return to the breeding colony in their first summer of life, and do not breed until they are at least four years old (see Chapter 2). Razorbills of two and three years which come to land in small numbers during June can be recognised by their small bills which sometimes lack the white stripe. Young Puffins also have small bills, with fewer ridges than the adults' bills, but this can only be seen reliably when the bird is examined closely, usually after being caught.

Kittiwakes are true cliff-nesting gulls although Herring Gulls will often breed on grassy ledges and the slopes of cliffs. Kittiwakes lay only two eggs as compared with the larger gulls' clutches of three and four, and this is an adaptation to their preferred feeding offshore. Other gulls which feed inland, on the coast or inshore are easily able to collect enough food to produce three or more eggs and to feed the chicks. The Kittiwake has to cope with more difficult and unpredictable feeding far from land

Figure 61

but here it has the advantage of avoiding competition for food with other gulls. Much of the courtship which takes place in April and May is carried out on the nest which the Kittiwakes build from grass gathered on the clifftops, especially near pools, cemented together with mud and guano onto a tiny ledge on sheer rock face or similar precarious site. The nest is the equivalent of the nesting territory defended by larger gulls and, if you watch closely, the birds can be seen using special calls and postures to display aggressively and ward off strangers, or to appease each other in order to strengthen the pair bond. The chicks which hatch in June are fed on partly digested fish and plankton regurgitated by the adult and taken straight from the gullet. This is an unusual habit as the chicks of other gulls feed from the parent's bill or, more often, from the ground; in the Kittiwake this is an adaptation to cliff nesting where ground is simply not available and the nest must be kept clean. When the chicks fledge after about a month in the nest, they are easily distinguished from the adults by the dark grey feathers in a W-shape across their wings, the black neck band and black bill. They do not breed until three years of age or more, and remain at sea for at least their first summer of life.

Fulmars and Manx Shearwaters also nest on cliffs. Like the auks, Fulmars do not build a nest and lay a single egg on a ledge in one of many different sites on high or low cliffs. They will also breed on sand dunes and inland on ruined buildings or walls and in fields. Fulmars occupy cliff colonies throughout the year and, apart from gulls, are often the only seabirds on the cliffs in winter. In April they undergo a pre-laying exodus from the colony in order to visit rich feeding grounds far offshore where food reserves are built up in preparation for the demands of the breeding season. The eggs hatch in late June and the chicks are covered with pale grey down. They grow quickly to the size of a football, fed by the parents on a mixture of stomach oils and predigested fish and plankton. The nestling period of two months is very long as the adults must collect food for themselves and their chicks further offshore than most other seabirds. The young Fulmars fledge in late August and early September.

Manx Shearwaters also lay a single egg and come to land only at night. They nest in burrows on the earthy parts of a cliff or on the clifftop, especially on offshore islands and their indescribable, eerie croaking is a

Figure 62 Manx Shearwaters at their burrow entrance on Skokholm, south Wales. Over 35,000 pairs of shearwaters nest on this small island and in summer the nights resound to their calls and whirring wings. They nest all over the island, burrowing into turf on the clifftops, amongst the bracken and in the old dry-stone walls.

characteristic feature of breeding colonies. Like all petrels, shearwaters forage far out to sea. Ringing has shown, for example, that birds from the island of Skokholm in south Wales feed regularly on sardine shoals in the Bay of Biscay, 500 to 900 kilometres away, whilst breeding. The birds lay in May and the chicks hatch about five weeks later but, like the Fulmar, they grow relatively slowly and must sometimes rely on their fat reserves to prevent starvation if the weather is rough and fishing difficult, so that the parents are delayed in returning with food. In late August or early September, about six to eight weeks after hatching, the young birds are deserted by the adults. They lose weight steadily for about ten days and when they emerge from the burrow, considerably thinner and without their nestling down, they are able to fledge and make their way, probably non-stop, to wintering grounds off Brazil. The navigational ability this journey requires is staggering. Moreover, the birds have excellent instinctive homing skills. The chicks sit out on the surface of the colony exercising their wings for a few nights before they actually fledge. During this time they are able to learn the position of the colony and their particular burrow so that they can return to it two or three years later as immature birds. Like most other seabirds, a vast majority of Manx Shearwaters settle in their natal colony to breed although they may visit other colonies during their summers as immature birds.

The Storm Petrel and the rare Leach's Petrel also breed in cracks and crevices on cliffs, especially in boulder scree, as well as in stone walls and ruined buildings. Like the Manx Shearwaters, storm petrels are entirely nocturnal at the breeding colony and are only occasionally seen as flitting, bat-like shapes against the sky. The birds sing from nest cavities with a repetitive whirring, hiccoughing call that has been facetiously described as resembling the sound of a fairy being sick. They are present in the colony from June until early October and have a similar breeding ecology to the other petrels.

The Gannet is another fairly rare seabird which breeds on cliffs and offshore islands. Gannets nest on the surface, often at high densities, and can be watched and studied with ease. Like other members of the family Sulidae, they have a repertoire of elaborate displays used to attract a mate, form and strengthen the pair bond, establish a nest site, drive away intruders and potential thieves of nesting material, appease the natural aggression of their mate and so on (see figures 63 and 74). These obvious and conspicuous displays are fascinating to watch and interpret and a Gannet colony is always a busy and addictively interesting place. The single eggs are laid in May in bulky nests of seaweed and guano, and when the chicks hatch in June they are naked and dark grey. They soon grow a thick covering of white nestling down but retain their black faces and bills. The speckled brown juvenile plumage is obtained before they fledge in late July onwards. When they first leave the colony, the young are often too heavy to take off from the sea and can be seen swimming away from the cliffs.

Shags lay in untidy nests of sticks and dried seaweed on cliffs and in caves. One to six eggs are laid and usually three chicks are reared and fed on partly digested fish from the parent's gullet, after frantic displays of begging by the chick. The breeding season is spread out and eggs are laid any time from April, or exceptionally March, to July. Cormorants build nests of mud and guano in dense colonies and their breeding season lasts from about April to August when generally two or three chicks are raised. Like those of the Shag, the chicks are tiny and naked when they first hatch and later grow a nestling down. They remain in or near the nest for four to five weeks.

Birds to be found nesting on the summit or slopes of offshore islands include most of the gulls – Herring, Great and Lesser Black-backed and Black-headed. The Great Black-backs are the predators of a seabird

Figure 63 A Gannet colony like this one on Bass Rock in the Firth of Forth is never still or quiet during the breeding season. The birds space their nests just out of range of their neighbours' bills. Some chicks here are in their white nestling down whilst the older ones have grown the speckled brown juvenile plumage and have nearly reached adult size. In the centre of the foreground an adult is sky-pointing with its bill. This display indicates it is about to leave the nest and is an important part of the nest relief ceremony; it prevents both birds mistakenly leaving the nest together which might enable neighbours to steal nest material, or a gull to take the egg or small chick.

colony and their kills are characteristically turned inside out and eviscerated. Like the other gulls, they regurgitate pellets of indigestible food remains and if these are collected and carefully taken apart, the gull's food can be identified. Oystercatchers, Shelduck, Velvet Scoter, Red-breasted

Figure 64 This Manx Shearwater has been killed by a Great Black-backed Gull and characteristically turned inside out. Great Black-backed Gulls are the main predators at seabird colonies; they kill adult birds up to the size of a Herring Gull and also take chicks and eggs.

Mergansers, Mallard, terns, skuas and passerines such as Skylarks, pipits and finches are all to be expected on the flat parts of the island. Birds other than seabirds which may also nest on the cliffs are Peregrines, White-tailed Eagles, Carrion Crows, Ravens, Choughs and Rock Doves which are typically cave nesters, Jackdaws and Starlings.

Islands are regularly used by migrants, mostly passerines, as stopping-off points for rest and food, especially in the kind of weather conditions which lead to the sudden obliteration of the cues, the stars and sun, needed for navigation. Storms at sea and high winds also cause 'falls', or the sudden appearance of flocks of small migrants, and rare or unusual species often turn up with them. In winter, wildfowl may use islands for shelter and feeding or for refuge from shooting on the mainland. Geese often winter on islands where there is sufficient grazing for them. Examples of this are the traditional wintering grounds of the Barnacle Goose on Islay, Scotland, or Inishkea and Mutton Island on the west coast of Ireland. The Barnacle Goose is said to be so named because of the belief that it hatched from barnacles on the shore; for this reason the geese were considred to be closer to fish than birds and were permitted food for Catholics on Fridays.

The birds out at sea

Common species From land, mainly during migration, gulls, terns, skuas, auks, Gannets, waders, shearwaters, seaducks and phalaropes. Out at sea, behind or near boats, Gannets, terns, gulls especially Kittiwakes, skuas, phalaropes, shearwaters and Little Auks. **Occasional species** From land, storm petrels, divers, passerines, some waders and ducks, swans, geese and birds of prey. At sea, almost any species as accidental visitors. **Best times** None; autumn migration from late August to mid-October best for seawatching from land. Heavy passage also visible from some coasts in spring from March to early May. Local movements between breeding colonies and feeding grounds during nesting season from May to early August.

Figure 65 The Great Shearwater is a scarce visitor to seas off northwest Europe. It breeds on the islands of Tristan de Cunha and Gough in the central south Atlantic and migrates in a huge loop around the Atlantic, arriving off the Newfoundland Grand Banks with the seasonal shoaling of capelin, and returning via the eastern Atlantic.

Identification of birds at sea is difficult because flocks are fast moving and hard to locate, and individual birds disappear easily behind waves. The best seawatching weather is rough and stormy, when the birds are closest to land, and this is also the wettest. A telescope is helpful for bird-watching at sea but needs experience before it can be used effectively. More than one pair of eyes is almost essential. Despite the difficulties, the birds seen at sea are usually interesting species or impressive in their numbers, and the process of migration can actually be seen.

Most species have characteristic flight patterns or wing beats which can be learnt fairly easily to aid identification. For example, shearwaters glide low over the waves in a rising and falling path, Gannets fly by alternate flapping and gliding, often in a V-formation, both auks and waders beat their wings fast and often fly low over the water, and terns use a typical buoyant flight with their bills pointing downwards if they are hunting. Many birds seen from land will be in flight apart from phalaropes, seaducks, divers, grebes, gulls and usually auks which are more often seen sitting on the sea. Remember to watch out for cetaceans and keep records of any sightings (see Appendix II).

Gannets and terns often fish close offshore, the former especially in rough weather. Both are spectacular in their precipitous dives into the sea and sometimes they can be seen emerging with fish in their bills. When hunting over shoals of fish, Gannets plunge-dive into small areas of water like raindrops and it is difficult to see how they avoid collisions. Skuas are sometimes seen pursuing an auk or tern or Kittiwake, usually birds smaller than themselves. The chase often lasts several minutes and

Figure 66 A Gannet plunge-dives. Just before it enters the water the bird straightens its wings behind it giving it an arrow-shape. No attempt is made to swim underwater but the momentum of the dive carries the Gannet deep down after its fish.

involves a fine display of aerobatics by both birds. Occasionally the skua will directly hit its target in an attempt to force it to drop or regurgitate its food. Birds as large as Gannets are driven down to the water by Great Skuas, and may even be submerged and drowned. In certain off-shore areas in autumn, usually out of sight of land, moulting flocks of auks can be seen accompanied by their young.

Figure 67 Herring Gulls are notorious scavengers and take advantage of fish and offal discarded from trawlers. The increase in the north Atlantic fishing industry during this century has provided gulls with a steady food supply and probably helped their population to increase. Gulls are rarely seen far from land unless following fishing boats.

Birds which regularly follow ships at sea looking for scraps of dis-carded rubbish or sewage or simply feeding on plankton stirred up by the wake, are shearwaters, Kittiwakes, storm petrels, Fulmars and, near land, Herring and Great Black-backed Gulls.

The birds on urban waterfronts

Common species Gulls, Oystercatchers, Cormorants, flocks of sea-duck. Nesting Herring Gulls and Kittiwakes. **Occasional species** Rare gulls, Turnstones, other waders and terns. Nesting Oystercatchers. **Best times** None. Roosts of gulls and sometimes waders largest in winter, and of terns in early autumn from July to August. Low tide for any mudflats on which there is intertidal feeding, and high tide for discharge from sewage outfalls. Also regular times when offal or rubbish is dumped.

A surprisingly large number and variety of birds can be seen in any seaside town or dock or rivermouth. The range of species depends on the habitats available. Gulls are attracted by offal from fish factories and the

Figure 68 Another way in which gulls have exploited Man is by feeding from rubbish tips. Here two Black-headed Gulls and an immature Great Black-backed Gull search for edible, and sometimes inedible, scraps.

sewage or rubbish produced in docks and cities and dumped at sea. Herring, Great Black-backed and Black-headed Gulls are the main scavengers, although recently Kittiwakes have also begun to feed in increasing numbers in urban estuaries and docks. Sewage outlets are particularly good places to see unusual or rare species of gulls. Large gull roosts form in winter on waste ground or in parks and playing fields near the sea. Oystercatchers and Redshanks often feed on urban grassland, especially playing fields, close to the coast. Turnstones are bold scavengers on harbour walls and sometimes feed, sparrow-like, around fish docks. Seaduck winter in huge flocks close to urbanised parts of several of the Scottish firths where waste grain discharged from distilleries via the sewage system provides rich feeding. The Seafield sewer south of Edinburgh on the Firth of Forth for example, attracted flocks of up to 40,000 Scaup, about thirty per cent of the total European wintering population, and huge numbers of Goldeneye with flocks of more un-usual species like Tufted Duck and Pochard. Unfortunately these flocks in industrial areas are especially vulnerable to oil pollution and the occasional discharge of toxic chemicals in the sewage.

Over-wintering flocks of species which are otherwise relatively rare and solitary, like grebes and divers, are found in urban estuaries and bays. One advantage of this is that the birds are often close enough to the shore to be clearly seen and identified.

Harbours and town seafronts often contain areas of intertidal mudflats or mud in reclamation pans which are almost never without waders of some kind. Numbers build up in autumn and winter. Before they are filled in, reclamation pans are particularly suitable as high tide roosting areas for waders, gulls and sometimes even terns. At one site in Dublin Bay, almost at the centre of a capital city, several hundred adult and juvenile terns can be seen roosting after the breeding season.

5 What else you can do

Records and field notes

Take a notebook with you when birdwatching on the coast and record all you see. Even small details which may seem irrelevant at the time may be important later. Keep special records of any unusual birds you see, including notes on appearance, behaviour, song and so on and, if possible, make a sketch of the bird. For every birdwatching trip record the date, weather and time as well as exactly where you went, what you saw, and any other relevant details such as the state of the tide. Here is a typical entry from a field notebook:

Date: *21st September*
Time of trip: *Morning*
High tide: *12.00 BST*
Weather: *Wind NNE, force 3, hazy sunshine becoming overcast. Sea moderately calm. Visibility good.*
Itinerary: *08.30–09.30 Wells harbour and Holkham beach and dunes. 23 Brent Geese grazing on Wells saltings; at least 7 juveniles. Also 2 Cormorants and 13 Mallard in harbour. 2 Redshanks feeding on low tide mud bank, plus about 30 Herring Gulls around fishing boat, 1 immature Iceland Gull with them. Little Grebe diving continuously in pool near Holkham car park. Flocks of gulls – Herring, Great Black-backed, Black-headed, about 150 total – offshore, feeding over sand banks on incoming tide. Waders feeding on muddy sand in channels leading to harbour; mainly Bar-tailed Godwits (about 30), Curlews (25–35), Dunlin (50–60), Redshanks (10+), Oystercatchers (12–15 on mud, flock of 34 flying past) and one Greenshank flushed from channel. 2 Ringed Plovers on upper beach watched taking sandhoppers from burrows in drier sand. Unidentified diver, Red-throated?, seen out to sea.*

Additional details which you should note where possible are the numbers and ages of birds in each species, where, how and upon what they were feeding, and any other behaviour such as nesting activity or direction of flight at sea. If you are making counts or other records for local or national surveys, you may need a special recording form or card. Ideally this should be designed for use in the field, but if it is large or easily torn or blown away, leave it at home and transfer the required information from your notebook to the form when you return. This has the added advantage of ensuring you retain a record of what you saw when the record form has been sent back to the survey organisers.

If possible, try to visit one convenient area of coast regularly throughout the year. This is particularly rewarding because you will be able to record the steady flow of migrants through the area, the arrival of breeding birds in spring, the events of the nesting period, the departure of breeding birds and their young, autumn migration, winter visitors, the build-up in numbers to a mid-winter peak, and the spring migration again. Your field notes will enable you to compare the birds present in different months, and even in the same season in different years.

Photographing birds

Almost since bird photography began in about 1860, the camera has been a two-edged sword to birds. Photography has played an important part in stimulating interest in birds and even in promoting their welfare. On the other hand, birds have sometimes suffered as a result of the few irresponsible photographers too intent on 'getting the picture' to care whether or not their subject was being disturbed. More than one rare bird has been quite literally hounded to death by a combination of bird-watchers and photographers. Discretion, rather than patience, is therefore the most valuable asset of a bird photographer.

There are basically two ways to photograph birds: either you go to them, or you can let the birds come to you. The first method involves stalking and the second generally requires the use of a hide. The early bird photographers used hides disguised as trees or animals such as cows (with six legs, two of them human) or hollow sheep. Nowadays a rectangular tent with at least enough room for a seat is preferred; these can be obtained from various firms, many of which advertise in the bird-watching magazines such as British Birds (see Appendix II). Experience has shown that the birds will not be suspicious of a hide providing a few simple rules are followed. First, the hide must be moved gradually to the required position, particularly if this is at a nest. This may take anything from a few hours to a few days, depending on the species to be photographed and the nature of the bird involved. This stage cannot be rushed, and if the bird shows signs of not returning to the nest, the hide must be removed immediately. Secondly, the photographer must be accompanied to the hide by another person who should then walk away as conspicuously as possible; very few birds can count and they will assume the hide is empty. The reverse procedure is followed when the photographer wants to leave as the sudden appearance of a human from the hide could make a nesting bird desert. Once inside the hide, the photographer must avoid any sudden movement or noise. A lens poking

Figure 69 Fulmars at nest sites on the Farne Islands, Northumberland. The birds occupy a site for several years before they actually breed. As with all other petrels no real nest is built, the Fulmars laying their single egg on the bare rock or earth.

through the front of the hide has to be moved very slowly and all equipment should be tripod-mounted. Many still cameras and virtually all ciné cameras need some form of soundproofing to muffle the noise of the shutter.

The relatively compact and lightweight 35mm single lens reflex (SLR) cameras have been widely available since the 1960s and have caused an increase in the popularity of bird photography. With their through-the-lens focusing and light metering, and interchangeable lenses, the SLR cameras are so versatile that they are particularly well suited to bird photography that involves stalking. The focal length of lenses varies from the standard 50mm to the extremely long telephoto lenses of 1,000mm or more. It is possible to buy a good quality telephoto lens relatively cheaply as its optical construction is simpler than that of other lenses, such as a wide-angle lens. Lenses with a focal length of more than 300–400mm must be used on a tripod, or a rifle grip, or otherwise rested on a firm support like a wall or rock to avoid camera shake in the photograph. A high shutter speed, at least 1/250th of a second, is needed when using a long lens hand held. The choice of both film and camera is now very much a matter of personal preference as most brands available are of excellent quality. Further detailed advice can be found in the publications listed in Further reading.

Reserves

There are many nature reserves around the coasts of Britain, Ireland and the other European countries, and these are all in good situations to attract seabirds, waders and other birds. The advantage of birdwatching on a reserve is that the habitat is specially managed by the warden and his helpers, usually volunteers, so that conditions are just right for birds. The reserve also provides protection from disturbance and, for some species, a sanctuary from shooting and so large numbers of birds gather there from surrounding areas. Hides are provided for observation without disturbance.

Reserves in Britain and Ireland (see figure 71) are in key areas of coast for either seabirds as at Bempton Cliffs, Yorkshire, and Grassholm Island, south Wales; waders on the Ribble estuary, Lancashire, and Minsmere and Havergate Island, Suffolk, or wildfowl as at the Wexford Slobs, southeast Ireland, and Slimbridge on the Bristol Channel. Some are of national importance and these are mostly managed by organisations like the Royal Society for the Protection of Birds and Nature Conservancy Council or the Forest and Wildlife Service in Ireland; many others run by county naturalists' trusts are of local importance and often just as interesting. To visit some reserves you will need a permit from the warden, and for the larger RSPB reserves you will have to book in

Figure 70 The basically simple plumage of the Razorbill is highlighted dramatically by white bars on the wing and beak and the white breast. The wing-bar is used in courtship. Razorbills come to land only during the breeding season.

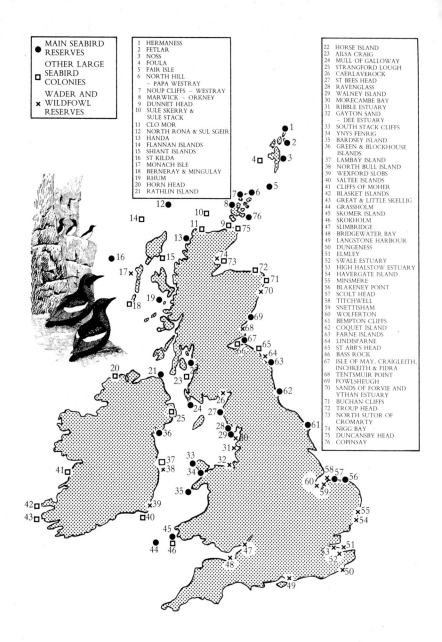

MAIN SEABIRD RESERVES
OTHER LARGE SEABIRD COLONIES
WADER AND WILDFOWL RESERVES

1 HERMANESS
2 FETLAR
3 NOSS
4 FOULA
5 FAIR ISLE
6 NORTH HILL – PAPA WESTRAY
7 NOUP CLIFFS – WESTRAY
8 MARWICK – ORKNEY
9 DUNNET HEAD
10 SULE SKERRY & SULE STACK
11 CLO MOR
12 NORTH RONA & SUL SGEIR
13 HANDA
14 FLANNAN ISLANDS
15 SHIANT ISLANDS
16 ST KILDA
17 MONACH ISLE
18 BERNERAY & MINGULAY
19 RHUM
20 HORN HEAD
21 RATHLIN ISLAND

22 HORSE ISLAND
23 AILSA CRAIG
24 MULL OF GALLOWAY
25 STRANGFORD LOUGH
26 CAERLAVEROCK
27 ST BEES HEAD
28 RAVENGLASS
29 WALNEY ISLAND
30 MORECAMBE BAY
31 RIBBLE ESTUARY
32 GAYTON SAND – DEE ESTUARY
33 SOUTH STACK CLIFFS
34 YNYS FENRIG
35 BARDSEY ISLAND
36 GREEN & BLOCKHOUSE ISLANDS
37 LAMBAY ISLAND
38 NORTH BULL ISLAND
39 WEXFORD SLOBS
40 SALTEE ISLANDS
41 CLIFFS OF MOHER
42 BLASKET ISLANDS
43 GREAT & LITTLE SKELLIG
44 GRASSHOLM
45 SKOMER ISLAND
46 SKOKHOLM
47 SLIMBRIDGE
48 BRIDGEWATER BAY
49 LANGSTONE HARBOUR
50 DUNGENESS
51 ELMLEY
52 SWALE ESTUARY
53 HIGH HALSTOW ESTUARY
54 HAVERGATE ISLAND
55 MINSMERE
56 BLAKENEY POINT
57 SCOLT HEAD
58 TITCHWELL
59 SNETTISHAM
60 WOLFERTON
61 BEMPTON CLIFFS
62 COQUET ISLAND
63 FARNE ISLANDS
64 LINDISFARNE
65 ST ABB'S HEAD
66 BASS ROCK
67 ISLE OF MAY, CRAIGLEITH, INCHKEITH & FIDRA
68 TENTSMUIR POINT
69 FOWLSHEUGH
70 SANDS OF FORVIE AND YTHAN ESTUARY
71 BUCHAN CLIFFS
72 TROUP HEAD
73 NORTH SUTOR OF CROMARTY
74 NIGG BAY
75 DUNCANSBY HEAD
76 COPINSAY

Figure 71 Birds can be watched almost everywhere on the coast but the main sites of international importance in Britain and Ireland include the large seabird colonies and the wader and wildfowl wintering areas on many of the estuaries. Most of these sites are now nature reserves.

advance through the society's headquarters (see Appendix II).

Particular mention must be made of the RSPB reserves at Minsmere and Havergate Island where 'scrapes' of shallow water and shingle islands are maintained for nesting terns, gulls, ducks, Avocets and other waders, and the Wildfowl Trust reserve at Slimbridge where thousands of geese, swans and ducks gather every winter to feed on saltings and meadows beside the Bristol Channel. If you have never visited either of these reserves you have a great experience in store, but bear in mind the time of year when planning a trip to these or any other reserves on the coast.

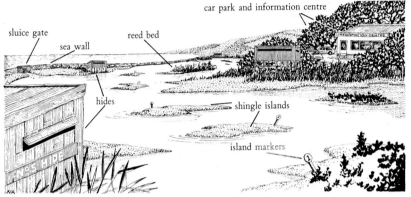

Figure 72 A typical coastal reserve situated on a lagoon or scrape behind the sea wall. Careful management of the surrounding vegetation and control of water levels by the sluice provide the best and most varied habitat for birds. Shingle islands can be constructed to attract nesting birds, especially terns. If necessary, the salinity of the water can even be maintained at a required level by pumping in fresh water so that optimum feeding conditions exist for birds, like Avocets, with specialised diet.

Seawatching

Watching and recording birds at sea, especially those on migration, is known as seawatching. Choose a point, headland or offshore island where the birds following the coast on migration have to come close to land and be prepared to watch for an hour or more at a time. Cliffs are ideal for seawatching from as an elevation of between twenty and a hundred metres above sea level improves one's vision of birds flying low over the sea. Seawatching can be carried out at any time of day when the light is good enough and, in theory, at any time of year. In practice, the migration season, especially in autumn from September to October, is the most productive time both in terms of the different species and the numbers of birds you will see. Stormy weather with rough seas often brings birds in close to land and provides good seawatching conditions. More advice on how to see birds at sea and which species to expect is given in Chapter 4.

When you become familiar with any particular part of the coast you will find that the different species seen vary widely in their abundance.

For example, a heavy passage of migrants may be represented by only ten Sooty Shearwaters seen passing in an hour, or by several hundred Kittiwakes within the same space of time. Watch out for solitary birds which will be easier to miss than flocks or skeins, and for birds resting on the surface, especially diving species which may stop to feed. Keep careful records of numbers and species seen in this way:

Duration of seawatch: *2½ hours, 09.30–12.00 BST*
Date & place: *3rd October, Skokholm Island*
No. of observers: *3*
Optics used: *10 × 50 binoculars, × 15– × 60 telescope*
Weather: *Wind SW, force 6–7. Visibility good, bright sunshine, very rough with heavy swell.*

Species seen	Passage to north	Passage to south	Nett passage
Gannet	1,1,5,3,6,1,1,1	1,15,2,1,32, 14,1	47 south
Kittiwake	4,3,1	5,7,9,3,1,23	40 south
Lesser Black-backed Gull	1,1	2,1,4,1,3,2	11 south
Herring Gull	2,3,9,3,1,15,2	10,1,3,7,1,4,10	1 south
Common Scoter	—	2,34	36 south
Unidentified seaducks	1	15	14 south
Razorbill	2,14,1,20	25,7,15,4,1	15 south
Unidentified auks	1,1	15,3,26,2	44 south
Terns – prob. Common	—	3,6,2,1	12 south
Waders – prob. Knot	—	47	47 south
Grey Phalarope	—	1	1 south

In this way it is easy to assess whether true migration is being recorded, or whether the same birds are being seen flying backwards and forwards. Birds are likely to do the latter for one of several reasons. Breeding birds from colonies nearby will visit feeding grounds and return to the colony with food several times daily during the nesting season from May to early August. Gulls and waders fly regularly between feeding and roosting grounds. Shearwaters often gather into huge rafts in the breeding season, and fly round and round an island where they nest in the late afternoon and evening whilst waiting to come to land. Local fishing boats or fish such as mackerel shoaling at the surface provide temporary abundant food sources for the birds and can upset migratory movements and seawatching.

Seawatching from a ship is complicated by the huge area of water in which the birds can occur. The most effective method of systematically collecting records is to select an area beside or behind the boat, ideally not much larger than the field of view of your binoculars or telescope, and search for birds only within this. As long periods of watching are tiring and one's powers of observation diminish accordingly, choose regular time periods, for example, ten minutes every half hour or fifteen minutes every hour, and stick to them. It is also important to record the approximate position of the ship and the speed at which it travels through the water for each period of observation, so that your records can be compared with those of other people on the ship, or on other ships in the area on the same date, or on different dates. Stand in the highest part of the ship in order to improve vision; this is often, with permission and to the crew's amusement, on the captain's bridge.

Seawatching will provide records of the numbers and variety of birds seen at sea from land which are of special interest when consecutive weeks of the autumn migration, or successive years are compared. However, the records are of greater value when they are fitted into the overall pattern of migration. Seawatching from land was especially popular amongst seabird enthusiasts in the 1950s and 1960s when most of the inshore migration routes were worked out. Even now, during autumn, observers around much of Britain and Ireland, especially the southwest, collect seawatching records, and these can be assembled into a composite record of migration. The British-based Seabird Group (see Appendix II) plays a part in collating, storing and occasionally analysing seawatching records collected from land and at sea. Anyone able to seawatch regularly should contact the Group and collect special instructions and recording forms. In addition, records of any cetaceans (whales, porpoises and dolphins) seen at sea are extremely valuable, and should be sent with full details to the Mammal Society (see Appendix II).

Birdwatching of this kind is useful as it helps to build up a picture of the distribution of birds at sea. Most seabirds become something of a mystery when they disappear after the end of their breeding season and information on the whereabouts, diet and behaviour of different species is badly needed. The main reason why this is important is that sea areas used by most birds are also of interest to conservationists. When pollution or offshore oil developments, for example, threaten to upset the ecological balance in one part of the sea, it is usually not known exactly whether or not the area is important to seabirds. In fact, some of the largest concentrations of birds at sea were first discovered, or their numbers only appreciated, when birds started being washed ashore after an oil pollution incident in the area. Information on the distribution of birds at sea is therefore vital in the planning of their protection. Several special studies and many years of research have already been conducted to try and locate birds at sea, especially in the northern North Sea. Much of the seawatching upon which this was based was carried out from specially charterd vessels. As this is impractical for long-term studies or for covering large geographical areas, the incidental seawatching records of birdwatchers on ships have to be relied upon to provide the necessary information. As long as these are collected in a standardised form and evaluated with care, they can give useful facts about birds at sea. If you plan to make a long sea journey or regular short distance crossings and are prepared to look for birds, please contact the Seabird Group for advice as your records could be of great value.

Surveys and censuses

Individual seawatching records become far more useful when they are combined with other people's observations and, similarly, records of birds seen on the coast can often be contributed to a census or survey being organised on a national, or even an international, scale. For example, between 1970 and 1975, the Birds of Estuaries Enquiry in Britain and its counterpart in Ireland, the Wetlands Enquiry, collected information on the species and numbers of birds (wildfowl, waders and gulls) on estuaries throughout Britain and Ireland. The enquiries were organised and sponsored jointly by the British Trust for Ornithology, the Royal Society for the Protection of Birds and the Wildfowl Trust, and the Irish Wildbird Conservancy respectively in the two countries, and the actual counts were carried out by a large number of volunteers. On selected dates each month the observers were instructed to count all the birds in 'their' estuary at high tide. Usually they worked in teams in order to cover the estuary thoroughly and to obtain a simultaneous count of all roosting birds within about an hour of high tide; this reduced the chance of duplication.

The results were collected and analysed at the BTO, and many valuable conclusions were drawn about the relative importance of different estuaries to birds of all species, and for some the areas of national or international importance. For example, as a result of the enquiries, thirty estuaries of international importance for waders, the average count totalling more than 20,000 birds, were listed; the twelve most important of these, each containing on average more than 50,000 birds, are marked on figure 71. The enquiry established Morecambe Bay in northwest England as the 'top' wader estuary with an average of 244,000 birds, and the Wash, East Anglia, second with 175,500 waders. Over twenty-five per cent of the European population of the pale-bellied subspecies of Brent Goose was found to winter on Strangford Lough in northeast Ireland, and over a third of the European dark-bellied Brent Geese to winter on the Essex estuaries in southeast England. Similarly, nearly thirteen per cent of the Scaup in northwest Europe were recorded on the Firth of Forth in southeast Scotland, and over seventeen per cent of the northwest European Pintail in the estuary of the river Mersey in north-west England. These facts backed up by hard data are vitally important to conservationists wanting to measure the relative importance of different estuaries, and they also help them to predict the effect of estuarine developments. In fact, the evaluation of the Brent Goose population wintering on the Essex coast, combined with other information collected in the early 1970s, was one of the main reasons for the conservationists' successful stand against the building of an airport at Foulness on the Maplin Sands.

The Birds of Estuaries Enquiry is one example of how individual counts of birds in different areas can be assembled into reliable, and therefore useful information. There are other current surveys to which birdwatchers can contribute. Populations of the commoner passerines in Britain are monitored through the Common Bird Census. This relies upon proved or suspected breeding records of species in a study area which is examined by the volunteer observer each year, mainly in April, May and June when the birds are breeding. Few coastal areas support large passerine populations, but if you are interested in contributing to this survey, write to the BTO (see Appendix II) for more information.

The Beached Bird Survey is organised by the RSPB and the Seabird Group in Britain, and by An Foras Forbartha in Ireland. Anyone who regularly visits a stretch of sandy or shingle beach, preferably one which tends to collect tide wrack and flotsam from the sea, can easily participate in this survey which also relies entirely on volunteers. Some of the birds which die at sea are washed ashore and can be found on suitable beaches such as those just described. By regular counts of corpses on beaches, the relative levels of mortality in birds at sea can be monitored. The number of oiled birds recorded indicates the degree of mortality caused by pollution and, since it started in the late 1960s, the Beached Bird Survey has recorded a wide range of mortality levels and oiling. Experiments in the Irish Sea in which marked gull corpses were dropped at known positions between Liverpool and the Isle of Man and then reported by the public when they were washed ashore, have shown that anything between forty-two and eighty-nine per cent of the bodies, depending on the strength and direction of prevailing winds, can disappear without trace. Thus many dead birds probably never float near enough to land to be beached so that the results of the Beached Bird Survey are used only as an indication of seabird mortality for long-term monitoring.

The main beached bird surveys take place in the winter months when bird mortality is heaviest. Once a year, at the end of February, surveys in Britain and Ireland coincide with similar counts on the beaches of Denmark, Holland, Belgium and northern France. This International Beached Bird Survey provides valuable comparative information on pollution and bird mortality for the coasts of much of northwest Europe. Volunteer recorders for the surveys are often needed, especially for the remote areas of coast in Britain, and for most of south and west Ireland. If you can help, write to the RSPB or An Foras Forbartha (see Appendix II).

Another way in which the national monitoring schemes can use your records is in the annual breeding seabird census, organised by the RSPB and the Seabird Group at colonies throughout Britain and parts of

Ireland. The earliest regular censuses of seabirds in Britain and Ireland were made for the Fulmar, and they have been carried out at ten-year intervals since the 1930s. James Fisher, who pioneered these studies, was also interested in the Gannet for which population estimates had been made since early this century. Being large and conspicuous birds with few breeding colonies, Gannets are relatively easy to census thoroughly. Complete counts of the British and Irish populations have been conducted at ten-year intervals since 1939. Kittiwakes have also been of interest for population censuses and ten-yearly surveys have been made since 1959. Elsewhere in Europe regular counts of seabirds are made in Norway where vast lengths of cliff are checked by light aircraft. A recently published atlas of breeding birds in France provides information on current seabird populations which are situated mainly in the northwest.

Counting seabirds accurately presents many problems. For example, some birds, like the auks, do not even build nests so that individual birds must be counted. Others, like the Manx Shearwater and storm petrels, are burrow or crevice nesters and visit land only under cover of darkness – they could hardly be more impossible to count! A complete census of all seabirds nesting on the coasts of the British Isles and Ireland was carried out in 1969. Organised by the Seabird Group and called 'Operation Seafarer', the survey involved over 1,000 volunteer observers, both amateur and professional. The results of Operation Seafarer are presented in a book by the chief organisers *The Seabirds of Britain and Ireland* (see Further reading) which is essential reading for anyone interested in seabirds. It is obviously impossible to repeat such a thorough and large-scale investigation annually and until counting techniques are refined to make population estimates accurate enough to detect quite small changes in numbers, it is not planned to repeat this exercise.

The auks are currently under particular threat from marine oil pollution which causes heavy mortality amongst all species and so their population levels are of special interest to conservationists. The Razorbill, Guillemot and Puffin, together with the two other cliff-nesting species which share the auks' colonies but are presently increasing in numbers, the Fulmar and Kittiwake, have been selected for annual population monitoring. Counts are needed from amateur and professional observers at one of two levels, depending upon the amount of participation they are prepared to offer. Counting these seabirds, especially the auks, accurately enough to detect population changes requires repeated fairly detailed and therefore time-consuming observations on

Figure 74 A greeting ceremony by a pair of Gannets on their nest. This mutual 'fencing' is part of courtship displays used to overcome natural aggression and strengthen the pair bond. (See also figure 63.)

successive days. These are usually limited to the height of the breeding season in June. Where colonies can only be visited briefly, perhaps only for one day, counts of this kind are impossible. Single counts give population estimates of low accuracy but are better than nothing for monitoring changes. At bird observatories, cliff nature reserves and some other areas, trained wardens are often present throughout the nesting season. These people are in an ideal situation to make repeated counts of breeding seabirds, yielding relatively accurate and so far more valuable results. If you visit a seabird colony regularly and are interested in counting seabirds, please contact the Seabird Group (see Appendix II).

Oiled, sick and injured birds

Sick or injured birds are often found on the coast, especially on beaches or the sheltered shores and waters of estuaries. Some seabirds are seen on or near land outside the breeding season only when they are sick. Unfortunately if a bird is so ill that it allows you to catch it, there is probably little hope for its survival. The usual causes are lack of food perhaps because of storms at sea, or weakness, disease, breakage of a leg or wing, poisoning by toxic chemicals (see Chapter 6) or oiling. An oiled bird tends to preen itself vigorously and so ingest oil from its feathers which causes slow poisoning and eventual death. Some birds which come ashore may have been oiled several weeks previously, and have removed all traces of oil except perhaps a tell-tale smear in parts they cannot reach like under the chin. They are often emaciated by the gradual poisoning effect of ingested oil, and frequently have oil residues in their droppings. A bird covered and clogged up with oil which comes ashore still fat may not have been affected long and may have not had time to ingest much oil; ironically its chances of survival are therefore considerably greater than those of an apparently clean bird. If you catch a sick bird on the beach and wish to care for it, you are most likely to succeed with a bird not suffering from oiling and some useful advice will be found in the publications listed in Further reading. Sick birds usually need nothing more than food and rest and can often be released again in less than week. The Royal Society for the Prevention of Cruelty to Animals (or the ISPCA in Ireland, see Appendix II) will give you essential advice on how to keep and care for injured seabirds, or if you prefer, they may take the bird from you.

Oiled birds present a different problem as they are very difficult to clean thoroughly and their chances of survival in captivity are low. In addition, oiling upsets the natural waterproofing of the feathers which is

Figure 75 A huge puffin colony covers the slopes of Mykines in the Faroe Islands. Puffins spend many hours standing around outside their burrows in the evenings, especially before they are old enough to breed. The bird on the right in the lower photograph has been colour ringed to indicate its natal colony. Colour ringing has shown that during their pre-breeding years, Puffins often visit other colonies and, although most return to the colony where they were born, some remain to nest elsewhere. The other bird is a Kittiwake.

so essential to a water bird (see Chapter 2), and even when the bird is clean, it may be slow to recover its waterproofing; some birds never do so. The longer a bird remains in captivity, the less chance it has of adapting to the wild on release. Generally, it is kinder to kill any oiled bird found rather than prolong its suffering by trying to clean it, but this is a matter of personal opinion. When really large numbers of oiled birds,

Figure 76 Although hardly recognisable as a bird, this is an oiled Gannet washed ashore following an oil spill at sea. This bird died immediately but many lightly oiled birds swim towards land. Sometimes the first indication of oil slicks at sea are dead and dying birds coming ashore.

both dead and alive, are washed ashore in Britain, the tragic victims of oil pollution at sea, the RSPCA may decide to collect and attempt to clean and rehabilitate the healthier birds. The association runs a rehabilitation centre at Little Creche in Somerset which is manned by volunteers and opened only in emergencies. Even at this professional centre the success rate with oiled birds is disappointingly low; sometimes as few as five or ten birds are finally released for every hundred treated. The operation involves only large numbers of birds from specific pollution incidents, and its aim is to return a great enough number of birds to the wild to have a significant effect upon their population levels.

Several organisations are concerned with monitoring oil pollution incidents around the British coast. You can help by looking out for oil or oiled birds or both on all beaches while birdwatching. If large amounts of fresh oil are seen coming ashore, contact the oil pollution officer of the local county council. If many oiled birds, whether dead or alive, are present, get in touch with the local office or headquarters of the RSPB or Nature Conservancy Council (see Appendix II) or both. Sometimes the first indication of oil spills at sea is the appearance of oiled birds on the beaches. Swift action in alerting the national organisations may mean that the necessary steps to find the spill, usually located by light aircraft or helicopter, to contain it with booms and clean it up by spraying chemicals or using suction pumps can be taken quickly and the further pollution of wildlife prevented.

Ringing and bird observatories

Ringing is the main way in which bird migration can be studied in the field, although several other techniques are used in the laboratory, especially to discover how birds navigate. Passerine migrants can be caught at bird observatories and waders, wildfowl and seabirds elsewhere on the coast. Passerines tend to migrate in flocks and, as birds in flocks are usually easier to catch than single birds, this is the time when most are ringed. Seabirds, by comparison, flock mainly at the breeding colony, and many are caught and ringed there. A breeding bird can be easily upset by being caught so great care is necessary when ringing seabirds. Waders and wildfowl, like passerines, are generally caught and ringed on migration. All birds in Britain and Ireland, and in most other European countries, are protected by law, and a special government licence is required by anyone handling wild birds. One ringing scheme covers both Britain and Ireland at present, and records are collected and stored on computer at the headquarters of the British Trust for Ornithology in Tring, Herts. Each ring carries the words INFORM BTO BRITISH MUSEUM NAT HIST LONDON SW7 together with a number which individually identifies the bird. When a dead ringed bird is found, the ring number is reported to the BTO via the British Museum (Natural History) in London, and gradually a composite pattern of migration for each species is built up. Sometimes a live bird is

Figure 77 A Storm Petrel caught at night in a breeding colony on Fair Isle, Shetland, is ringed using special ringing pliers. The plastic string in the foreground holds spare rings.

caught and, after its ring number is read, released again; this record is known as a retrap or control.

Up to 1978, the following numbers of seabirds had been ringed in Britain and Ireland, and recovered dead.

	Number Ringed	Number reported afterwards	%
Fulmar	36121	449	1.2
Manx Shearwater	222396	2970	1.3
Storm Petrel	114735	741	0.6
Leach's Petrel	4797	40	0.8
Gannet	40222	2423	6.0
Cormorant	24962	4756	19.1
Shag	66469	5427	8.2
Great Skua	34680	911	2.6
Arctic Skua	5254	113	2.2
Great Black-backed Gull	21994	1098	5.8
Lesser Black-backed Gull	72728	4239	5.8
Herring Gull	136776	8936	6.5
Common Gull	17714	592	3.3
Black-headed Gull	151555	7116	4.7
Kittiwake	51317	1148	2.2
Common Tern	64280	1203	1.9
Arctic Tern	65335	872	1.3
Roseate Tern	19240	321	1.7
Little Tern	5540	73	1.3

Sandwich Tern	101755	2698	2.7
Razorbill	39673	1211	3.1
Guillemot	33333	903	2.7
Black Guillemot	3239	43	1.3
Puffin	70557	602	0.9

As can be seen from these figures the proportion of ringed birds re-covered in each species varies widely. Both the storm petrels are small and spend most of their time far out at sea so that there is little chance of ringed birds being found dead. Their recovery rate is low and less than one in a hundred are heard of again after ringing. Other seabirds with recoveries totalling less than two per cent of those ringed are the terns, long-distance migrants often far from land and Kittiwakes and Puffins which are both comparatively pelagic members of their respective families. By comparison, Cormorants and Shags are recovered more often than any other seabird; nearly one fifth of all Cormorants ringed are found and reported after death. This is probably because they are large birds, easily noticed, and also because they are unprotected at certain times of year and shot in many areas by fishermen fearing com-petition for fish stocks. Recovery rates are also high in gulls.

Ringing also provides a method of studying how long birds live and whether they move around between breeding colonies. Retraps of live birds are particularly useful here. Colour ringing is sometimes used to enable a bird to be individually identified or identified as belonging to a certain age group – both useful in studies of breeding biology. Coastal birds are typically long lived as explained in Chapter 2; ages of fifteen to twenty years or more are quite usual for many seabirds, even the smallest storm petrels, also eight to ten years for seaducks and ten or fifteen years for many of the waders.

There are several different ways of catching birds on the coast for ringing. The main ones are as follows:

Mist nets are very fine and almost invisible and they are made specially for birds. The netting is strung in loose folds or pockets between taut shelf strings looped around long bamboo poles which are sunk into the ground and kept upright with guy ropes. The birds fly into the nets and become lightly tangled in the pockets for long enough to be removed for ringing. Mist nets are used for catching many species of birds on the coast (and bats!) including all waders, Puffins and storm petrels.

The **cannon net** catching technique was developed for use on ducks and roosting waders, and it has been used successfully on a wide variety of birds including gulls feeding on rubbish tips and some passerines. Cannon nets are large, usually about twenty by twelve metres, with ropes along one of the longer edges attached to heavy metal projectiles; this is known as the leading edge of the net. The net is set by pegging the other long edge, known as the baseline, securely to the ground and by furling the netting into a pile over it. The projectiles are placed into the

Figure 78 A cannon net is fired over a flock of roosting waders on Dee estuary. This method enables large numbers of birds to be caught and ringed at one time. The baseline and cannons are obscured by smoke, and the leading edge with the projectiles attached is in the air.

barrels of four cannons which are dug into the ground behind the baseline and connected up by an electric circuit with the firing box situated in a hide about fifty metres away. When catching waders the nets are used in pairs or lines and are set on a beach, spit or coastal field where a high tide roost is situated. On spring tides the birds' intertidal feeding areas are completely covered by water and numbers using the roosts are at a maximum; these are the best times for cannon netting. The hide overlooks the potential catching area covered by the nets, and when conditions are right, the cannons are fired electrically. The projectiles carry the net over the birds' heads and as many as a thousand or more can be caught at one time, although usually catches are smaller. The birds are covered up immediately after the catch until they can be extracted from the nets. They are then allowed to stand in special hessian keeping cages before being ringed, weighed, measured, examined for wing moult and then released.

Heligoland traps are large funnel-shaped wire cages, built over

Figure 79 This heligoland trap on Fair Isle, Shetland, is built over the only trees on the island. Migrants and roosting finches are attracted to the cover and can be driven, from right to left, into the catching box at the apex.

isolated patches of vegetation in parts of the coast where many migrants make landfall, usually at bird observatories. The birds gather in the cover to feed and shelter and can be driven into the funnel, ending up in a small box at the top where they can be caught. Many different migrants, mostly passerines, are caught in heligoland traps including some ground-living species like Water Rails and Corncrakes.

Wader traps are wire netting cages designed like lobster pots. They are placed on mud or other areas where waders feed regularly, and when the bird walks into the trap of its own accord, it is unable to find its way out again.

The traditional way of catching seabirds, particularly Puffins, Fulmars and Gannets, on the Faeroe Islands and in Iceland (mainly the Westmann Islands) is by using the **fleyg net** which traps birds in flight. It is designed like a huge butterfly net on a long pole and operated by an experienced catcher from a projecting point on the cliffs where many birds fly past. Enormous numbers of seabirds were once caught by this method and used for food; it is also useful for trapping birds for ringing.

There are various other methods of trapping breeding birds on the nest, but these are not widely recommended. Most seabirds can be

Figure 80 This eighteenth-century print shows an artist's impression of seabird fowling. The man holds a fleyg net, which would have been more commonly used on a clifftop outcrop or ledge, with which to catch flying birds. Ropes were used to reach ledges on the cliffs where seabird chicks could be collected. In the background, the gap between the clifftop and an offshore stack has been bridged so that the men can collect the eggs and chicks of Gannets and Guillemots.

approached on the nest and both adults and young caught for ringing but care must be taken to avoid disturbance.

Ringing gives one a good chance to see birds in the hand and it makes an interesting and rewarding hobby in addition to birdwatching. However, several years' comprehensive training is necessary before the required ringing licence (already mentioned) can be obtained. To watch people ringing birds on the coast or to participate yourself, contact the BTO who should be able to put you in touch with local ringers, or visit a bird observatory. Ringers usually, but not always, act in teams when trying to catch waders, wildfowl or seabirds. Most of the estuaries in Britain and the Shannon estuary in the west of Ireland have active wader ringing groups. Seabird ringing is confined to relatively few colonies (see figure 81) where nesting birds are accessible without disturbance or danger. In all cases the BTO acts as the coordinator of ringing projects.

Migrating birds, especially passerines, often stop off to feed and rest at vantage points on the coast along their route. Headlands, spits and offshore islands usually provide a first landfall for migrants crossing the sea or following the coastline. Birds move in flocks and set out on migration together when weather conditions are favourable. If the weather changes, large numbers of them are forced to land and many may be blown far off course. R. M. Lockley was one of the first to realise that bird migration could actually be observed at strategic points around the coast including his island home of Skokholm off the south Wales coast. He established the first bird observatory in Britain there in 1933 with the aim of studying migration through careful visual records and ringing. The first heligoland trap was built, copying a design that Lockley had seen in operation on the German island of Helgoland. Since then a number of bird observatories have been set up at vantage points on the coast where large numbers of migrants make regular landfall, and thirteen are operating at present (see figure 81). Thousands of common migrants, some rare ones and a few vagrant species are caught in heligoland traps and mist nets and ringed each year. Many bird observatories are also excellent places for seawatching so that the passage of birds along the coast at sea can be recorded. Visual records of the numbers and species of birds passing through each observatory, together with information from ringing recoveries, combine to provide much valuable data on the patterns and timing of migration for many different species. Bird observatory records are also of value for the study of moult and pre-migratory weight gains.

Visitors are welcome at all bird observatories and most offer hostel-type accommodation. More information on the British and Irish bird observatories can be found in a book called *Bird Observatories in Britain and Ireland* (see Further reading). This gives a description of each observatory, its birds, activities, available accommodation and so on. Several observatories are noted for their breeding seabirds during the summer

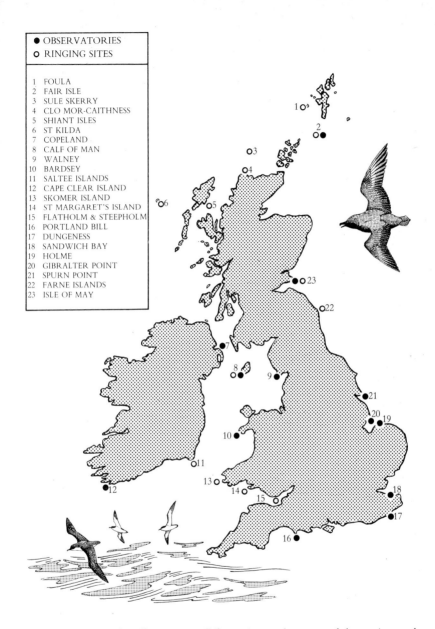

● OBSERVATORIES
○ RINGING SITES

1 FOULA
2 FAIR ISLE
3 SULE SKERRY
4 CLO MOR-CAITHNESS
5 SHIANT ISLES
6 ST KILDA
7 COPELAND
8 CALF OF MAN
9 WALNEY
10 BARDSEY
11 SALTEE ISLANDS
12 CAPE CLEAR ISLAND
13 SKOMER ISLAND
14 ST MARGARET'S ISLAND
15 FLATHOLM & STEEPHOLM
16 PORTLAND BILL
17 DUNGENESS
18 SANDWICH BAY
19 HOLME
20 GIBRALTER POINT
21 SPURN POINT
22 FARNE ISLANDS
23 ISLE OF MAY

Figure 81 Ringing takes place at many different sites on the coast and the species caught depend largely on the type of habitat. The map shows coastal sites where large numbers of seabirds are ringed regularly, and the bird observatories where many passerine migrants are ringed. Wader ringing takes place on nearly all the British estuaries and some of the larger Irish ones.

months but the best time to visit them is in the spring or autumn during the birds' migration. At these times of year one never knows what sorts of birds will turn up; sudden 'falls' of migrants or the appearance of unusual or rare species blown off course are both regular occurrences. Anyone interested in coastal birds and migration will undoubtedly find a stay at any bird observatory well worthwhile.

Other studies

So many aspects of the ecology of coastal birds have been studied using different techniques and with intriguing results, that I can only recommend the books and papers listed in Further reading. The various research projects cover such aspects as feeding: what the birds feed on and where, how much nourishment they need to survive and how their weight changes during the year; breeding: where, when and how birds breed, population censuses and changing numbers, nesting success, survival and population dynamics; moult and other subjects such as the distribution of birds outside the breeding season. Many aspects of bird biology can be studied on a simple level by any birdwatcher by, for example, watching birds feeding and identifying their diet, by counting birds and estimating breeding population sizes, or by recording nesting birds' behaviour. The methods used by research workers and reported in their publications can often be scaled down and applied by anyone to the birds seen regularly on the coast. Ideas of how to study birds and the kind of questions to ask yourself about them can also be gained by joining the various ornithological and birdwatching organisations, listed in Appendix II for Britain and Ireland but also in existence in other European countries.

6 Conservation of coastal birds

The conservation of all animals, including birds, hinges upon information about numbers and changes in population sizes. The species requiring conservation are identified partly by the fact that their numbers are changing, usually declining, and the success of conservation efforts is gauged by their effect upon populations. This is why the national survey and censuses of birds on the coast, which are described in Chapter 5, are so essential to conservation as they provide the facts with which conservationists must work.

The different species of birds found in coastal habitats vary enormously in their comparative abundance or rarity; the two measurements are quite separate. For example, nearly all the Golden Plovers which breed in Iceland winter in Ireland so that they are very common there. The total Irish wintering population frequently exceeds 200,000 birds. In fact, the Icelandic Golden Plover is an isolated subspecies and relatively rare, and the Irish birds represent just about the only wintering population of birds from this part of the species' range. Similarly, several birds, including the Roseate Tern, Peregrine and Avocet, are considered rare breeders in Britain and Ireland. (The Avocet is confined to Britain.) Actually these species are merely at the edge of their ranges and nest abundantly elsewhere.

In addition to this need to consider counts and estimates in an international context, there are all the problems connected with accurate census techniques and the interpretation of results. Special care is necessary when dealing with migratory species. On the Wash in eastern England, for example, flocks of waders pause on migration or during winter to feed on invertebrate-rich mudflats. The total mid-winter count recorded by the Birds of Estuaries Enquiry (see page 123) averages about 172,000 waders. Many years of ringing and retrapping ringed waders, carried out by the Wash Wader Ringing Group, has enabled the actual number of birds passing through the Wash to be calculated, which is far in excess of those present at any one time. It was found that at least 228,000 waders visit the Wash every year, making it of even greater international importance than the Bird of Estuaries Enquiry suggested.

In addition to the waders and wildfowl on the coast, the populations of nesting seabirds are unique. The coasts of Britain and Ireland alone hold at least five-and-a-half million breeding seabirds, as the results of

Operation Seafarer in 1969 showed. (These figures are estimates because most seabirds are impossible to count accurately.)

More than 100,000 pairs:	Razorbill, Guillemot, Puffin, Gannet, Kittiwake, Herring Gull, Fulmar, Manx Shearwater, and (probably) Storm Petrel.
More than 10,000 pairs, but less than 100,000:	Lesser Black-backed, Great Black-backed, Black-headed and Common Gulls, Shag, Arctic, Common and Sandwich Terns.
More than 1,000 pairs, but less than 10,000:	Black Guillemot, Cormorant, Arctic and Great Skuas, Little Tern, and (probably) Leach's Petrel.
Less than 1,000 pairs:	Roseate Tern.

Large numbers of all gulls, with the exception of Kittiwakes, also nest inland and were not covered by Operation Seafarer. Significant proportions of the world populations of the Gannet, Shag, Great Skua, Storm Petrel and Razorbill, and much of the northwest European population of nesting Lesser and Great Black-backed Gulls, Sandwich and Roseate Terns are found in Britain and Ireland.

Until the middle of the last century, no birds were protected in

Figure 82 The human population of St Kilda in the last century with the annual crop of Fulmars. Life on remote islands was maintained by the harvest of seabirds. Gannets, Fulmars, Puffins and, to a lesser extent, Guillemots and their eggs were collected for food and preserved by salting or drying. Discarded seabird guts were used for compost and their feathers exported to the mainland or used to stuff mattresses. Stomach oil from the thousands of Fulmars slaughtered each summer provided the St Kildans with their only source of light through winter.

Britain or in any other European country. A flourishing trade in birds' eggs and feathers which were used for trimming hats and clothes existed, and many species were killed for eating. On remote islands like St Kilda, far off the west coast of Scotland, and the Faeroe Islands, the people depended mainly on birds and their eggs for survival. Large numbers of seabirds, mainly Gannets, Fulmars and Puffins, were killed, dried and salted or stored for food during the winter months. Fulmar oil, skins and feathers were put to a whole variety of uses by the St Kildans, rather in the way that the Eskimos of Greenland still use Little Auks. In 1869, pressure of public opinion, mostly from members of an organisation founded in the mid-nineteenth century (now known as the Royal Society for the Protection of Birds) and others protesting against the slaughter of seabirds and the exploitation of their eggs, led to the passage of the first bird protection bill through the British parliament; this dealt only with seabirds. More laws soon followed and gradually seabird numbers began to recover from persecution by Man. Gannets, gulls, terns, skuas and auks have all increased in numbers during the present century; the Gannet, for example, at about three per cent a year and the Kittiwake at around four per cent.

In the seventeenth century Fulmars bred only in northwest Iceland and on St Kilda and there are remains on St Kilda to suggest that they nested there are early as the sixth century. During the eighteenth century, Fulmars suddenly began to spread out around the coasts of Iceland reaching the Faeroes in 1839 and eventually Norway early this century. The St Kildan population also expanded and in 1878 Fulmars began nesting in Britain; they colonised Ireland in 1911, and later even northwest France. The reason for this virtual explosion of the north Atlantic Fulmar population is far from clear. It has been attributed to one or more of the following: genetic changes in the original northern birds which adapted them to life in warmer waters further south; or to climatic changes affecting the birds' food supply; or to the increasing amounts of food, in the form of offal, made available to Fulmars by the whaling industry and, when over-fishing all but wiped out the north Atlantic whale stocks, by the commercial fishing fleets. The real cause may be a combination of all these factors, but there is no doubt that Fulmars are continuing to increase and to spread, as their recent invasion of the almost cliffless southeast coast of England shows.

The Kittiwake has also increased in northwest Europe. Its breeding population in Britain and Ireland is known to have nearly doubled in size between 1959 and 1969. Fewer new areas were colonised during the increase so that it took place relatively undetected. One reason for the birds' success may be the adoption of scavenging habits particularly by feeding behind fishing boats and, most recently, even in urban estuaries. Numbers of the other gulls have also increased spectacularly throughout Europe and in many other parts of the world, due to the growing protection and the provision of more and more sources of artificial

Figure 83 Until St Kilda was evacuated in 1930, traditional methods were used to catch breeding seabirds including snares and fleyg nets. Huge numbers of nestling Gannets, Fulmars and auks were collected from the precipitous cliffs by men on ropes made of straw or horsehair. Here a St Kildan stands on a clifftop with his catch of Fulmars.

food. Like the Kittiwake, the Herring Gull and, to a lesser extent, the Lesser and Great Black-backed Gulls sometimes make use of buildings

Figure 84 Urban gulls have adopted the habit of nesting on buildings in seaside towns as this roof-top Herring Gull site shows. Breeding success is often low, but the birds are guaranteed a food supply close by.

for nesting, usually near supplies of rubbish, offal or sewage. Some of the Herring Gulls nesting on Skokholm, off the south coast of Wales, feed their chicks on offal or rubbish collected on the mainland, in particular at the nearby Milford Haven fish docks. Colour ringing and a study of breeding productivity and chick growth of the gulls on Skokholm showed that birds which feed on the fish docks, and bring artificial foods to their chicks, reared more young to fledging age than the birds which were rarely or never seen in the fish dock, and probably therefore fed mostly at sea. Similar findings have been suggested by studies in Holland.

The higher breeding output of birds with access to artificial foods, and the ability of young gulls to breed for the first time at a younger age in an expanding colony, discovered by long term studies at several different sites, have enabled gull populations to increase dramatically since the 1940s. Artificial food supplies have also aided the birds' over-winter survival and encouraged many of them, especially the Lesser Black-backed Gull which was once entirely migratory, to remain in northwest Europe during winter. As breeding colonies grow, gulls compete successfully for nesting space with other species, often pushing out terns and ducks.

Some seabirds have decreased in numbers in the last fifty years, despite continuing and increasingly effective protection. The terns suffer badly from disturbance whilst nesting; Sandwich Terns especially

Figure 85 Guillemots return to the breeding colony early in spring and join huge flocks or rafts on the sea below the cliffs. Much of the pairing or re-pairing with the mate of the previous year, and courtship, takes place on the water.

will panic and completely desert a colony if disturbed early in the breeding season. Each species has its own requirements for nesting habitat, and they all need safety from ground predators like cats, rats, stoats and escaped mink which can cause heavy losses. High tides often wash over low-lying banks or beaches where terns nest, further reducing the production of young. Areas suitable for nesting such as offshore shingle banks may be swept away completely by winter storms, and coastal areas sufficiently remote and peaceful for nesting terns become increasingly rare as reclamation and development occur. Breeding is therefore a precarious process and tern populations are especially vulnerable to breeding failure in successive years. In addition, large numbers of terns, apparently Roseate Terns in particular, are trapped on their wintering grounds in west Africa. They are taken in hundreds by small boys, sometimes for food but more often for fun, caught skilfully in snares or on a baited fishing line when they dive. How much mortality is caused in this way cannot be measured or even estimated by ringing recoveries because, without the educational programme to back up the ringing schemes in Europe, most rings from dead birds are not reported. Possibly as a result of this, Roseate Terns are rapidly approaching near extinction in northwest Europe. Other causes, such as the chemical pollution of breeding birds during the 1960s (see below), and low breeding productivity in successive seasons coupled with the loss of nesting habitat have also undoubtedly played a part. Roseate Tern numbers in Britain and Ireland, which in 1969 held over eighty per cent of the total European population, have declined from about 3,000 pairs in the late 1950s, and nearly 2,500 pairs in 1969, to about 750 pairs ten years later.

The auks have also decreased since the 1940s, probably mainly in the 1960s, but are currently just about stable or increasing in parts of their ranges. The Puffin populations in northern Britain are particularly difficult to sort out. The birds declined steadily in numbers during the 1960s on the west coast of Scotland, although the earlier, rather subjective records of 'Puffins darkening the sky' with their numbers are of little use for comparison. Existing assessments of Puffin numbers before 1940 are scarce and rarely quantitative. Research during the 1970s has shown that numbers have been stabilising and are increasing slightly in northwest Britain, and are rising fast in the northeast. For example, only a few pairs of Puffins nested on the Isle of May in southeast Scotland up to 1960; over 3,000 pairs bred there in 1975, and the colony is continuing to grow. This rate of increase is impossible without immigration

Figure 86 In this group of Guillemots on a nesting ledge some of the chicks are nearly old enough to fledge or go down to the sea. The adult on the right is bridled, a genetic variety far less common in the south of the species' range, and one on the left is colour ringed.

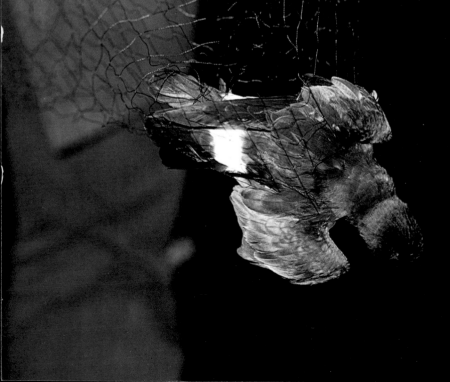

but Puffins, like other seabirds, were not originally considered to move around between breeding colonies very often. Recent research, however, is showing that more and more species do so to a considerable degree. Colour ringing of very large numbers of Puffins in northern Britain has proved that some birds move to breed on the Isle of May from the Farne Islands further south, where increasing numbers have caused a shortage of space. Some birds have moved between colonies elsewhere, such as St Kilda and Great Saltee, southeast Ireland, and a few have gone north to Iceland and the Faeroe Islands from Britain.

The disastrous effect that small increases in adult mortality can have on population dynamics in auk species was explained in Chapter 2. Oiling, shooting, accidental snaring in fishing nets and starvation in stormy weather, all regularly kill large numbers of birds at sea. Auk populations are also severely affected by mass mortality caused by marine pollution.

The chemical pollution of rivers, and so estuaries and the sea, has affected both seabirds and coastal birds in most countries of northwest Europe. Direct poisoning by residues of pesticides used on the land which drained into the river Rhine literally decimated the tern populations nesting in its estuary during the 1960s and these are only now beginning to recover. Various industrial chemicals, especially those in the polychlorinated biphenyl group (PCBs) which are involved in tanning and many other manufacturing processes, are discarded in effluent from factories and reach estuaries and the sea. They pass through invertebrates and fish to concentrate at the top of the food chain, in birds. They are deposited mainly in the body fat and also accumulate in the liver and brain. Analysis of large numbers of seabirds' eggs and livers has shown that concentrations of PCBs and other pollutants such as pesticide derivatives and heavy metals are highest in birds from enclosed sea areas such as the Irish Sea, and inshore species like Cormorants and Shags, although every species examined contained toxic chemicals at confusingly variable concentrations. When birds come under stress, perhaps because stormy weather makes feeding difficult, or if they are replacing feathers during the annual moult, the fat reserves are utilised. The toxic chemicals then enter the bloodstream and have a debilitating effect on the bird. As an indirect result of toxic chemical contamination, bird mortality is artificially high when conditions are difficult and this has its effect on population levels. During the autumn of 1969, over 15,000 unoiled seabirds were found dead and dying on the coasts of the Irish Sea and the total mortality must have exceeded 50,000 birds. Although the exact cause of this incident was never established, toxic

Figure 87 The Storm Petrel breeds in thousands at colonies in northwest Europe but the birds are impossible to count accurately as they nest deep in rock crevices and visit land only at night. Birds in flight at the colony can be caught in mist nets (below) and ringed but the chance of a ringing recovery, a report of the bird after death, is low because Storm Petrels are so small and live far out at sea.

chemicals were thought to be mainly responsible.

The Peregrine is another coastal species affected by chemical pollution, this time by pesticide derivatives. Peregrines, beautiful and spectacular birds of prey, were once widespread breeders throughout much of Britain and Ireland, especially on the coast. Contamination via the food chain by the residues of DDT, then widely used in agriculture, led to the birds producing unusually thin-shelled eggs. Breeding success became minimal as eggs broke, the birds' behaviour grew abnormal and clutches were deserted. By the mid 1960s only a handful of pairs were left in Britain although the Irish population, subject to less poisoning through the more limited use of pesticides, fared a little better. Since the main groups of chemicals likely to contaminate the environment have been restricted in use or banned altogether by law, numbers of Peregrines and other birds affected by toxic chemicals have recovered.

Oil pollution has already been mentioned as a cause of death in auks, but it can also affect other birds. Some of the oil at sea originates from natural seepage from the earth's crust, but far more is spilt from ships. Accidental collisions and groundings can cause spills of cargo oil from tankers; these are often heavy crude oils which form thick sludge when beaten up by waves and wind, and irretrievably contaminate the delicate intertidal zone on being washed ashore. Fuel oil is also often spilt accidentally from the ship's bunkers, and this can cause the gravest pollution of birds at sea. Deliberate oil spillage is difficult to detect as amounts involved are usually quite small. Tankers need to carry water as ballast when their tanks are empty and, before the existence of international laws against marine pollution, this oily water was dumped as the tanker approached port. The system of 'load-on-top' is now used to separate the oil and water but its efficient operation depends on the provision and conscientious use of storage tanks for oily water in onshore depots. Some tankers still surreptitiously dump ballast water or jettison waste oil at sea and the accumulative pollution this causes produces chronic mortality among seabirds.

The large, well publicised accidents which cause vast oil slicks at sea also take their toll of birds. The incidents involving the *Torrey Canyon*, the *Christos Bitas* and the *Amoco Cadiz* are but a few examples. The exploitation of oil fields under the sea and associated developments onshore also cause problems for birds for, wherever large amounts of oil are handled, spills always occur. Between late December 1978 and mid-March 1979, nearly 5,500 oiled birds were found in northeast and south Shetland following spills from the *Esso Bernica* at the Sullom Voe oil terminal and other ships at sea. Among the casualties of the *Esso Bernica* spill were 146 rare Great Northern Divers; others were mainly Shags, Eider, Long-tailed Duck and auks. An estimated sixteen per cent of the islands' Black Guillemot population was killed in that one winter. Birds which live in flocks such as the wintering Great Northern Divers in the Shetland Isles are particularly susceptible to oiling as a single slick can kill huge numbers. Auks are also very vulnerable when they gather into flocks to moult, and the large concentrations of all kinds of seabirds near breeding colonies in summer are a special risk.

Many wildfowl flock in vast numbers to the Waddenzee, an enormous area of tidal mudflats off the coasts of Holland and northwest Germany. In autumn most of the duck there, including 100,000 Shelducks, are moulting, and are therefore temporarily flightless. In winter the numbers increase as geese, swans, and ducks arrive from all over Europe, not to mention the numerous waders which also use the area. The Waddenzee is of vital international importance and is situated precariously at the very edge of the North Sea shipping lanes. Perhaps the worst oil pollution record belongs to the coasts of Denmark, especially to the Kattegat channel where ships collide with monotonous regularity. This area and the southern Baltic is used by well over a million seaducks, mainly Common and Velvet Scoters, in winter. In the latest of a whole series of pollution incidents in January 1979, over 35,000 ducks are known to have been oiled.

Mortality caused by oil has a particularly drastic effect on birds at the edge of their range where breeding populations tend to be small. A few auks nest in southwest England, the Scilly and Channel Islands and in northwest France, mainly on Les Sept Iles, at the edge of the Puffin and Razorbill's breeding distribution, and towards the southern limit of the Guillemot. Large numbers of birds that would otherwise have bred in these colonies were killed by oil from the *Torrey Canyon* in 1967, and again eleven years later, when their numbers were just beginning to recover, by oil from the *Amoco Cadiz*.

So far only the threats to the birds themselves have been considered. Coastal birds are also affected by the destruction of their habitat which removes valuable feeding grounds and, in some cases, breeding areas. Many parts of the coast of Europe are still wild and unspoilt, like the cliffs and storm-bound islands lashed by the Atlantic, and the spacious mudflats and saltings stretching as far as the eye can see. Naturalists, and birdwatchers in particular, are the first to appreciate and enjoy such areas, but town planners, ambitious farmers, engineers and the promoters of tourism condemn them as being unproductive 'wasteland'. Reclamation of coastal habitat for agriculture, urban development or water storage using sea walls, dykes and polders, has been carried out extensively in many countries, especially the low-lying ones around the southern North Sea. When one considers the enormous importance to birds of certain estuaries, for example, the planning of such schemes must be the urgent concern of conservationists. Nature reserves are needed to ease the pressure on remaining habitats; as different areas disappear under the bulldozer or behind sea walls the birds crowd into any suitable places still left to them. A certain amount of development is necessary of course. Land is needed for agriculture and sometimes for housing but there is no reason why planning cannot be carried out with

Figure 88 An aerial view of the Lincolnshire coast of the Wash. In the foreground saltmarsh, threaded with drainage channels, leads to mudflats and the sea. Behind the sea wall more saltmarsh gradually drying out is being reclaimed to give farmland like that in the distance. The whole of this area would once have been saltmarsh, windswept and alive with a wide variety of birds.

regard for the environment, and areas set aside as nature reserves to go some way towards compensating the birds for their loss of habitat.

Other, more localised threats to estuaries include pollution by effluents from factories and uncontrolled rubbish dumping. The natural vegetation can be altered by the planting of cord grass initially to stabilise the mudflats. The hybrid forms which are particularly fertile are introduced (see page 21), and the subsequent spread of a thick mat of grass can clog the estuary. Sand removed from dunes and gravel from shingle spits upsets the natural succession of habitats (see Chapter 1) and destroys bird haunts. Dune slacks are scoured by the wind following the removal of sand, making it impossible for gulls and terns to nest there, or shingle banks, suitable for breeding birds, are washed away by artificially diverted tidal flow. Elsewhere in the world, Man has had a spectacular and disastrous effect on many endemic seabirds and landbirds on oceanic islands by introducing domestic animals like pigs, dogs, ferrets, cats, goats and rabbits. These destroy the birds' habitat by grazing, trampling and digging, or are direct predators of species previously completely without enemies. In northwest Europe mink farms are often situated on islands; one was proposed but fortunately banned for Papa Westray in the Orkneys, a tiny island holding a breeding colony of up to 17,500 pairs of Arctic Terns. On the coast of Sweden mink have practically decimated Razorbill and Black Guillemot populations.

The bird protection laws in Britain (1869–1954) were one of the first major conservation achievements. A similar Wildlife Act was passed in Ireland in 1976, and most other European countries have followed suit. Many have also signed and ratified the International Convention for the Protection of Endangered Species (1963) which, of course, includes birds. International laws preventing oil pollution at sea and in docks have been passed, often helped by pressure from the public stimulated by conservationists. Organisations which should be mentioned here in this respect are the International Union for the Conservation of Nature, based in Geneva, and the International Council for Bird Preservation, with headquarters in London. Fines are now imposed for all spills of oil although in many cases they are hardly large enough to act as a deterrent. It is impossible to enforce the laws at sea but chronic pollution does seem to have lessened since the late 1950s and 1960s when the impact of mass transport of oil by sea was first felt.

Possibly the largest contribution has been made not by international laws and bodies, but by the efforts of those concerned locally and nationally to educate others about all aspects of wildlife conservation. Organisations like the Royal Society for the Protection of Birds, the Irish Wildbird Conservancy, the British Trust for Ornithology, and others mentioned in Chapter 5, have helped in this way. Education of both teachers and children, conservation planning, farming and wildlife advice, enforcement of bird protection laws, research on populations and habitat management, administration of reserves and membership promotion are all undertaken by the RSPB, the largest conservation organisation in Europe, whose membership is now approaching the one million mark. The BTO coordinates national surveys, ringing projects and the collection of many other kinds of information on birds. Local naturalists' trusts and an increasing number of county councils around Britain have appointed conservation officers and established nature reserves, often on the coast, in areas of promising habitat which are sometimes saved from industrial development or reclamation as a result. These in turn provide good opportunity for educating the large numbers of visitors which arrive to use the hides and other facilities.

Habitat management on coastal reserves creates the best conditions for nesting birds and may attract birds from other areas outside the reserve. On the RSPB reserves at Havergate and Minsmere in Suffolk the water levels in shallow pools inside the sea walls are artificially controlled to give plenty of shingle banks for nesting birds and shallow water of the correct salinity for an abundance of the Avocet's favourite food, a brine shrimp. Avocets nest in only a few other places in Britain; they were once fairly widespread breeders in small numbers but disappeared, probably mainly because of interference by Man. For a hundred years none bred anywhere in Britain or Ireland and then in 1938 a site in County Wexford, southeast Ireland, was colonised briefly, and the birds moved to

Figure 89 Sometimes a simple notice like this one at Pagham Harbour, Sussex, is all that is needed to reduce casual disturbance to terns and waders nesting on a beach. Although the terns have suffered badly through loss of habitat as peaceful beaches become holiday resorts and the coastline is altered by reclamation, they will often nest on specially prepared habitat on coastal nature reserves.

breed in Suffolk in 1947. Protection from disturbance by humans and the removal of potential predators on reserves have also helped terns; almost all existing tern colonies of any size in Britain are on reserves.

Conservationists sometimes have quite the reverse role to play as some species are in need of population control. The steady increase of all six kinds of gulls breeding in Britain and Ireland has already been mentioned. The same species have also undergone population increases, triggered by protection, in all other European countries and in North America. The growing numbers of the larger gulls, especially Herring Gulls, have caused problems in areas where they foul drinking water when roosting on reservoirs, or where they nest noisily and untidily on buildings. At many breeding colonies their gradual usurpation of habitat from the more timid terns has provided cause for concern. The smaller Black-headed Gulls seem to attract nesting terns, in particular Sandwich Terns, into their midst when breeding, possibly because the gulls' noisy and successful mobbing of potential predators near the colony is to the terns' advantage. Culling of breeding birds under Government licence by the use of narcotic baits was carried out in the early 1970s on the Isle of May, southeast Scotland for several successive years with only partial success in reducing the gull population as many birds simply moved away to breed in other colonies nearby. These included the islands of Fidra and Inchmickery where the RSPB runs its own gull control programme in order to preserve nesting habitat for terns. The age of first breeding in the Herring Gulls left on the Isle of May dropped to about three years instead of the more usual four or five, and as a result the numbers are now threatening to build up again quickly.

What you can do

You may feel that you would like to help in the conservation of birds on the coast and elsewhere. The first recommendation is to join one of the national conservation organisations listed at the back of the book and described in this chapter. You will benefit from the literature you receive and the access you have to reserves, films, lectures and so on and, on the other hand, the organisation will gain valuable membership and funds from you. These organisations are mostly registered charities operating without financial support from the government; this is essential for the freedom of their work, and it means that they depend on the continuing support of their members.

Secondly, you can join your local naturalists' trust which needs your support for the same reasons and which will inform you about local reserves and other activities. Volunteers are often needed for management work, wardening of nesting birds, or the supervision of visitors on reserves, and you may be able to help.

Thirdly, you can support the conservation of coastal habitats and their birds by keeping in touch with events on local, national and perhaps even international scales. Information from the organisations already mentioned will help you do this. Anyone can help bring pressure to bear on planning departments or, via their local representatives, on governments against the unnecessary or irresponsible destruction of coastal areas and for the control of coastal pollution by enforcement of local and national laws. You can help by collecting the information which conservationists need to argue their case, and by contributing to national surveys and censuses (see Chapter 5).

Finally, by being aware of the problems and aims of wildlife conservation, you can educate others.

Appendix I Scientific names of birds mentioned in text

Audouin's Gull   *Larus adouinii*
Arctic Skua   *Stercorarius parasiticus*
Arctic Tern   *Sterna paradisaea*
Avocet   *Recurvirostra avosetta*
Barnacle Goose   *Branta leucopsis*
Barrow's Goldeneye
                    Bucephala islandica
Bar-tailed Godwit   *Limosa lapponica*
Bewick's Swan   *Cygnus columbianus*
Black-bellied Sandpiper *see* Dunlin
Blackbird   *Turdus merula*
Black Guillemot   *Cepphus grylle*
Black-headed Gull   *Larus ridibundus*
Black-necked Grebe
                    Podiceps nigricollis
Black-tailed Godwit   *Limosa limosa*
Black Tern   *Chlidonias niger*
Black-throated Diver   *Gavia arctica*
Black-winged Stilt
                    Himantopus himantopus
Brent Goose   *Branta bernicla*
Broad-billed Sandpiper
                    Limicola falcinellus
Brünnich's Guillemot   *Uria lomvia*
Carrion Crow   *Corvus corone*
Caspian Tern   *Sterna caspia*
Chough   *Pyrrhocorax pyrrhocorax*
Common Gull   *Larus canus*
Common Sandpiper *Tringa hypoleucos*
Common Scoter   *Melanitta nigra*
Common Tern   *Sterna hirundo*
Cormorant   *Phalacrocorax carbo*
Corncrake   *Crex crex*
Curlew   *Numenius arquata*
Curlew Sandpiper   *Calidris ferruginea*
Dotterel   *Charadrius morinellus*
Dunlin   *Calidris alpina*
Dusky Redshank *see* Spotted Redshank
Eider Duck   *Somateria mollissima*
Fairy Tern   *Gygis alba*
Fulmar   *Fulmarus glacialis*
Gannet   *Sula bassana*
Glaucous Gull   *Larus hyperboreus*
Goldeneye   *Bucephala clangula*
Golden Plover   *Pluvialis apricaria*
Goosander   *Mergus merganser*
Great Auk   *Pinguinus impennis*

Great Black-backed Gull
                    Larus marinus
Great Crested Grebe   *Podiceps cristatus*
Great Northern Diver   *Gavia immer*
Great Shearwater   *Puffinus gravis*
Great Skua   *Stercorarius skua*
Green Plover *see* Lapwing
Green Sandpiper   *Tringa ochropus*
Greenshank   *Tringa nebularia*
Grey Crow *see* Hooded Crow
Grey Heron   *Ardea cinerea*
Grey Phalarope   *Phalaropus fulicarius*
Grey Plover   *Pluvialis squatarola*
Gull-billed Tern   *Gelochelidon nilotica*
Guillemot   *Uria aalge*
Gyrfalcon   *Falco rusticolus*
Harlequin Duck
                    Histrionicus histrionicus
Hen Harrier   *Circus cyaneus*
Herring Gull   *Larus argentatus*
Hooded Crow   *Corvus corone cornix*
Iceland Gull   *Larus glaucoides*
Jackdaw   *Corvus monedula*
Kentish Plover
                    Charadrius alexandrinus
Kestrel   *Falco tinnunculus*
King Eider   *Somateria spectabilis*
Kittiwake   *Rissa tridactyla*
Knot   *Calidris canutus*
Lapwing   *Vanellus vanellus*
Leach's Petrel   *Oceanodroma leucorhoa*
Lesser Black-backed Gull   *Larus fuscus*
Linnet   *Carduelis cannabina*
Little Auk   *Alle alle*
Little Grebe   *Tachybaptus ruficollis*
Little Gull   *Larus minutus*
Little Ringed Plover   *Charadrius dubius*
Little Stint   *Calidris minuta*
Little Tern   *Sterna albifrons*
Long-tailed Duck   *Clangula hyemalis*
Long-tailed Skua
                    Stercorarius longicaudus
Mallard   *Anas platyrhynchos*
Manx Shearwater   *Puffinus puffinus*
Marsh Harrier   *Circus aeruginosus*
Meadow Pipit   *Anthus gustavi*

Mediterranean Gull
  Larus melanocephalus
Merlin   *Falco columbarius*
Montagu's Harrier   *Circus pygargus*
Mute Swan   *Cygnus olor*
Oystercatcher   *Haematopus ostralegus*
Pectoral Sandpiper   *Calidris melanotos*
Peregrine   *Falco peregrinus*
Pintail   *Anas acuta*
Pochard   *Aythya ferina*
Pomarine Skua   *Stercorarius pomarinus*
Puffin   *Fratercula arctica*
Purple Sandpiper   *Calidris maritima*
Raven   *Corvus corax*
Razorbill   *Alca torda*
Red-breasted Merganser
  Mergus serrator
Red-necked Grebe   *Podiceps grisegena*
Red-necked Phalarope
  Phalaropus lobatus
Redshank   *Tringa totanus*
Red-throated Diver   *Gavia stellata*
Ringed Plover   *Charadrius hiaticula*
Rock Dove   *Columba livia*
Rock Pipit   *Anthus spinoletta*
Roseate Tern   *Sterna dougallii*
Ruff   *Philomachus pugnax*
Sabine's Gull   *Larus sabini*
Sanderling   *Calidris alba*
Sandwich Tern   *Sterna sandvicensis*
Scaup   *Aythya marila*
Shag   *Phalacrocorax aristotelis*

Shelduck   *Tadorna tadorna*
Shore Lark   *Eremophila alpestris*
Short-eared Owl   *Asio flammeus*
Shoveler   *Anas clypeata*
Skylark   *Alauda arvensis*
Slavonian Grebe   *Podiceps auritus*
Slender-billed Gull   *Larus genei*
Snipe   *Gallinago gallinago*
Snow Bunting   *Plectrophenax nivalis*
Sooty Shearwater   *Puffinus griseus*
Sooty Tern   *Sterna fuscata*
Sparrowhawk   *Accipiter nisus*
Spotted Redshank   *Tringa erythropus*
Starling   *Sturnus vulgaris*
Steller's Eider   *Polysticta stelleri*
Storm Petrel   *Hydrobates pelagicus*
Teal   *Anas crecca*
Temminck's Stint   *Calidris temminckii*
Tufted Duck   *Aythya fuligula*
Turnstone   *Arenaria interpres*
Twite   *Carduelis flavirostris*
Velvet Scoter   *Melanitta fusca*
Water Rail   *Rallus aquaticus*
Whimbrel   *Numenius phaeopus*
White-billed Diver   *Gavia adamsii*
White-tailed Eagle   *Haliaeetus albicilla*
White Tern   *see* Fairy Tern
Whooper Swan   *Cygnus cygnus*
Wigeon   *Anas penelope*
Wood Sandpiper   *Tringa glareola*
Woodpigeon   *Columba palumbus*

Appendix II Useful addresses

An Foras Forbartha Teoranta The National Institute for Physical Planning and Construction Research (for the Beached Bird Survey in Eire), St Martin's House, Waterloo Road, Dublin 4.

Army Birdwatching Society, c/o Lt. Col. N. Clayden, MOD Defence Lands, 4 Tolworth Towers, Surbiton, Surrey.

British Birds, c/o Macmillan Journals Ltd., 4 Little Essex Street, London WC2R 3LF. This journal is produced every month for birdwatchers; it includes papers on identification, up-to-date birdwatching news and photographs.

British Ornithologists' Union, c/o Zoological Society of London, Regent's Park, London NW1 4RY. This is the senior ornithological society in Britain. Members receive the journal *Ibis* four times a year and can attend the annual conference and other meetings.

British Trust for Ornithology, Beech Grove, Tring, Herts. Members receive the newsletter six times a year and four issues of the journal *Bird Study*.

Ringers receive the journal *Ringing and Migration*, and the *Ringers' Bulletin*. The BTO coordinates the ringing scheme in Britain and Ireland and its staff and the ringers analyse and publish the results. The Trust also issues licences, nets, rings and other ringing equipment. It organises a wide range of national surveys including the Common Bird Census and Birds of Estuaries Enquiry.

County Naturalists' Trusts. These own and manage reserves and organise meetings and outings for members. Addresses are available from local libraries or by sending an s.a.e. to The Society for the Promotion of Nature Conservation, The Green, Nettleham, Lincs LN2 2NR.

Irish Society for the Prevention of Cruelty to Animals, 1 Grand Canal Quay, Dublin 2.

The Irish Wildbird Conservancy, c/o Royal Irish Academy, 19 Dawson Street, Dublin 2. Members receive a regular newsletter. An annual conference is held jointly with the RSPB, alternating between Northern Ireland and the Republic of Ireland. The IWC owns and manages several reserves including one seabird island.

The Irish Wildlife Federation, c/o 8 Westland Row, Dublin 2. Members receive newsletters. The IWF arranges lectures for its members and educational programmes for teachers and school children on birds and all aspects of conservation.

The Mammal Society (for sighting of cetaceans), 62 London Road, Reading, Berks RG1 5AS.

Nature Conservancy Council (for reports of oiled birds), 19 Belgrave Square, London SW1X 8PY, or see telephone directory for local and regional offices.

Royal Air Force Birdwatching Society, c/o Sq. Leader D. Hollin, RAF Wyton, Cambs.

Royal Naval Birdwatching Society, c/o 23 St David's Road, Southsea, Hants. Members receive the journal *Sea Swallow*.

Royal Society for the Prevention of Cruelty to Animals (for advice on the care of sick birds), The Manor House, Horsham, Sussex RH12 1HG, or see telephone directory for local officers and centres.

Royal Society for the Protection of Birds, The Lodge, Sandy, Beds SG19 2DL. Members receive the magazine *Birds* four times a year and have access to over sixty reserves throughout Britain and Northern Ireland including at least eighteen on the coast. The RSPB provides national film shows and annual members' conferences; local members' groups organise birdwatching trips, lectures and film shows.

Seabird Group, c/o RSPB, as above. Members receive newsletters three times a year and the *Seabird Report* biennially. The Group coordinates and funds many amateur studies of seabirds including national surveys like Operation Seafarer; it also maintains close liason with other seabird groups in South Africa, Australia and the Pacific.

Wildfowl Trust, Slimbridge, Glos GL2 7BT. Members receive the quarterly journal *Wildfowl* and have access to numerous wildfowl reserves throughout Britain.

Young Ornithologists' Club, c/o RSPB, as above. Members are birdwatchers up to eighteen years of age. They receive the magazine *Bird Life* six times a year and a more regular newsletter. Many field trips, films, talks and competitions are arranged by local members' groups.

Further reading

Identification guides to birds

Bruun, Bertel and Singer, Arthur. *The Hamlyn Guide to the Birds of Britain and Europe*. Hamlyn, 1970, rev. ed. 1978.

Campbell, B. and Watson, D. *Birds of Coast and Sea. Britain and Northern Europe*. Oxford University Press, 1977.

Hayman, P. and Burton, P. *The Bird Life of Britain*. Mitchell Beazley in association with the RSPB, 1976.

Heinzel, Hermann, Fitter, Richard and Parslow, John. *The Birds of Britain and Europe with North Africa and the Middle East*. Collins, 1972.

Jonsson, Lars. *Birds of Sea and Coast*. Penguin, 1978.

Peterson, Roger, Mountfort, Guy and Hollom, P. A. D. *A Field Guide to the Birds of Britain and Europe*. Collins, 1954, 4th ed. 1979.

Prater, T., Marchant, J. H. and Vuorinen, J. *Guide to the Identification and Ageing of Holarctic Waders*. BTO Field Guide, No. 17, 1977.

Saunders, David. *RSPB Guide to British Birds*. Hamlyn, 1975.

Tuck, Gerald and Heinzel, Hermann. *A Field Guide to the Seabirds of Britain and the World*. Collins, 1978.

Birdwatching guides

Conder, Peter. *RSPB Guide to Birdwatching*. Hamlyn, 1978.

Gooders, J. *How to Watch Birds*. André Deutsch, 1975; Pan Books, 1977 (paperback).

Gooders, J. *Where to Watch Birds*. André Deutsch, 1967, rev. ed. 1974; Pan Books, 1977 (paperback).

Gooders, J. *Where to Watch Birds in Europe*. André Deutsch, 1970, rev. ed. 1974; Pan Books, 1978 (paperback).

Reference books

Cramp, S. (Chief Ed.) *Handbook of the Birds of Europe, the Middle East, and North Africa. Vol. 1 Ostrich to Ducks*. (Covers divers, grebes, petrels, cormorants, Gannet and wildfowl.) Oxford University Press, 1978.

Durman, R. (Ed.) *Bird Observatories in Britain and Ireland*. T. & A. D. Poyser, 1976.

Flegg, J. J. M. *Binoculars, Telescopes and Cameras for the Birdwatcher*. BTO Field Guide, No. 14, 1972.

Harrison, J. M. *Bird Taxidermy*. David & Charles, 1976.

Hickman, M. and Guy, M. *Care of the Wild Feathered and Furred*. Wildwood House, 1980.

Hollom, P. A. D. *The Popular Handbook of British Birds*. H. F. and G. Witherby, 1952, rev. 4th ed. 1968.

Marchington, J. and Clay, A. *An Introduction to Bird and Wildlife Photography*. Faber & Faber, 1974.

Warham, John. *The Technique of Bird Photography*. Focal Press, 1973.

Identification guides to life on the shore and at sea

Barnes, R. S. K. *Natural History of Britain and Northern Europe: Coasts and Estuaries* (one of 5 vols. in this series). Hodder & Stoughton, 1979.

Barrett, J. and Yonge, C. M. *Collins Pocket Guide to the Seashore*. Collins, 1958.

Campbell, A. C. and Nichols, J. *The Hamlyn Guide to the Seashore and Shallow Seas of Britain and Europe*. Hamlyn, 1976.

Evans, P. G. H. *Guide to Identification of Cetaceans in British Waters*. The Mammal Society, 1976.

Fraser, F. C. *British Whales, Dolphins and Porpoises*. British Museum (Natural History), 1969, 5th ed. 1976.

Hepburn, I. *Flowers of the Coast*. Collins, 1952.

McLusky, D. *Ecology of Estuaries*. Heinemann Educational Books, 1971.

Ranwell, D. S. *Ecology of Salt Marshes and Sand Dunes*. Chapman & Hall, 1972.

Distribution and biology of coastal birds

Cramp, S., Bourne, W. R. P. and Saunders, D. *The Seabirds of Britain and Ireland*. Collins, 1974, 2nd ed. 1975.

Fisher, J. *The Fulmar*. Collins, 1952.

Fisher, J. and Lockley, R. M. *Seabirds*. Collins, 1954.

Holdgate, M. (Ed.) *The Seabird Wreck of 1969 in the Irish Sea*. National Environmental Research Council, 1971.

Hutchinson, C. D. *Ireland's Wetlands and their Birds*. Irish Wildbird Conservancy, 1979.

Lack, D. *The Natural Regulation of Animal Numbers*. Oxford University Press, 1954, 2nd ed. 1967; 1970 (paperback).

Lack, D. *Population Studies of Birds*. Oxford University Press, 1966; 1969 paperback).

Lockley, R. M. *Shearwaters*. J. M. Dent, 1942.

Lockley, R. M. *Puffins*. J. M. Dent, 1953.

Lockley, R. M. *Ocean Wanderers: Oceanic Birds of the World*. David & Charles, 1974.

Mead, C. *Bird Ringing*. BTO Field Guide, No. 16, 1974.

Murton, R. K. *Man and Birds*. Collins, 1971.

Nelson, B. *The Gannet*. T. & A. D. Poyser, 1978.

Nelson, B. *Seabirds their biology and ecology*. Hamlyn, 1980.

Perry, R. *At the Turn of the Tide*. Lindsay Drummond, 1943; reprinted, Croom Helm, 1973.

Saunders, D. *Seabirds*. Hamlyn, 1971.

Sharrock, J. R. *The Atlas of Breeding Birds in Britain and Ireland*. T. & A. D. Poyser for the BTO and the IWC, 1967.

Sparks, J. *Bird Behaviour*. Hamlyn, 1969.

Tinbergen, N. *The Herring Gull's World*. Collins, 1953.

Tuck, L. *The Murres, their Distribution, Populations and Biology*. Canadian Fish and Wildlife Service, 1960.

Seabird islands

Buxton, J. and Lockley, R. M. *Island of Skomer*. Staple Press, 1950.

Darling, F. F. *Island Years*. George Bell, 1940. (Outer Hebrides)

Eggeling, W. *The Isle of May*. Oliver & Boyd, 1960.

Harris, M. and Murray, S. *Birds of St Kilda*. Institute of Terrestrial Ecology, 1978.

Lockley, R. M. *The Island.* Penguin, 1980. (Skokholm).

Perry, R. *Lundy, Isle of Puffins.* Lindsay Drummond, 1940.

Perry, R. *Watching Seabirds.* Croom Helm, 1975. (Reprint of above book with additional information on Fair Isle.)

Roche, R. and Merne, O. J. *The Saltees: Islands of Birds and Legends.* O'Brien Press, 1977.

Sharrock, J. R. (Ed.) *The Natural History of Cape Clear Island.* T. & A. D. Poyser, 1973.

Steel, T. *The Life and Death of St Kilda.* The National Trust for Scotland, 1965; Fontana, 1975 (paperback).

Williamson, K. *The Atlantic Islands: A Study of the Faroe Life and Scene.* Routledge & Kegan Paul, 1970.

Williamson, K. and Boyd, J. Morton. *St Kilda Summer.* Hutchinson, 1960.

Acknowledgements

Colour photographs

Aquila: R. Kennedy 9 top, Richard Mills 54 top; Ardea: G. K. Brown 10 bottom, John Daniels 144 bottom, Richard Vaughan 9 bottom, 126 top, 144 top; Biofotos: Heather Angel 115, 125 bottom; Frank Blackburn 71; Bruce Coleman: Giorgio Gualco 116, R. K. Murton 54 bottom, R. B. Tulloch 143 top; David Hosking 89 top; Eric Hosking 35; Bryan Sage 53 bottom, 72, 89 bottom, 90, 125 top, 126 bottom, 143 bottom; Paul Sterry 10 top, 36, 53 top.

Black-and-white photographs

Aquila: Dennis Green 94, T. Leach 86, R. T. Mills 78, E. K. Thompson 95; Ardea: 133, R. J. C. Blewitt 96, Anthony and Elizabeth Bomford 21, J. B. and S. Bottomley 91, 141, P. Germain 108, John Mason 148, Tom Steel 138, David and Katie Urry 82, 84, 100, 102, 103, 110, Richard Vaughan 33, 81, 85, 92, 97, 98, 104, 111; Biofotos: Heather Angel 19, 22, 23, 106; Anthony and Elizabeth Bomford 109 left and right; Andrew Cleave 150; Bruce Coleman: Gordon Langsbury 93; Eric Hosking: 7, 31, 39, 41, 76, 83, 101, Niall Rankin 140; Chris Johnson 34, 132 top; Clare Lloyd 42 bottom, 107; Iain S. Robertson 130, 132 bottom; Royal Society for the Protection of Birds: Hansgeorg Arndt 32, Jan van de Kam 77, William S. Paton 29, Michael W. Richards 42 top, 128.

Index

Page references in italic refer to illustrations; page references in bold refer to recognition details of bird groups in Chapter 3.

Auks, 26, *27*, 28, 29, 37, 42, **67–8**, 99–102, *102*, *103*, 108, 109, 145: Great, 26; Little, 41, 68, 108, 139; *see also* Guillemots, Puffin, Razorbill
Avocet, *30*, 37, 59, 60, 137, 149–50

Beaches, 53: sandy, 6, *12*, 17–18, *18*; birds of, 75–80; shingle, 6, *12*, *18*, 22–3, *22*; birds of, 95–6
Binoculars, use of, 70, 73–4, *73*
Binomial nomenclature, 47–9
Bird families and species, classification of, 48–9; *see also* individual families
Bird observatories, 129, 134–6; map of *135*
Bird protection, 75, 129, 138–9, 149, *150*
Birds of Estuaries Enquiry, 122–3, 137
Body, adaptation of, 27–31; names of parts, *47*
Bonxie, *see* Great Skua
Breeding productivity, 43–4, *44*
British Trust for Ornithology, 122, 129, 134, 149, 153
Brood patch, *95*
Bunting, Snow, 69, 80
Buzzards, 26, *58*

Camouflage, 25, 33, *36*, 41, 42, *42*, 77, *78*
Censuses, 122–7, 136; Common Bird, 123
Cetaceans, 109, 121, 154
Chough, 107
Cliffs, 6, 23–4, *71*, *72*, *100*: birds of islands and, 99–108
Coastline, formation of, 7–8, *8*; importance to birds of, 6–7, 11–13, *13*
Colour ringing, 84, *126*, 131, 141, *143*, *see also* Ringing
Cord grass, *Spartina*, 21: hybrid, 22, 148
Cormorants, 26, *30*, 32, *32*, **52**, **55**, *55*, 89, 105, 131, 145
Corncake, 133
Crows, 69: Carrion, 69, 86;

Hooded (Grey), 69; *see also* Jackdaw
Curlew, 28, *30*, 60, 93, 98

Deferred maturity, 43
Displays: anti-predator, 31, *31*, 41, *41*, 84, *84*; courtship, 32–3, *33*, *125*; nest relief, *106*; territorial, *54*, 77–8, *77*, *82*, 93, *93*
Divers, 15, 26, 28, 37, **50**: Black-throated, 50, *50*; Great Northern, 50, 146; Red-throated, 50, 113; White-billed, 50
Dotterel, 63
Ducks, 28, 32–3, *33*, 34, 37, **56–8**: dabbling, 58; diving, 57–8; Harlequin, 58; Long-tailed, 57, 92, 146; Tufted, 58, 112
Dunlin, *9*, 28, *39*, 40, *43*, 47, 49, *59*, 62, 93–4

Eagles, 26; White-tailed, 59, 107
Eclipse plumage, 34, 57
Eider, 29, 41, *42*, 57, 80–1, 146: King, 57; Steller's, 58
Estuaries, 6, 11, *12*: main sites, *118*, 122–3; importance to migrants of, *39*, 40

Falcons, **58–9**, *58*
Feathers, function of, 26, *27*, 31–3, *32*, *34*, *47*; *see also* Moult
Feeding, of coastal birds, 37–8: avoidance of competition in, 28–9, *28*, 42–3; bill adaptation in, 28–9, *28*, 29, *30*; ducks, 81, 88, 92, *94*; gulls, 76, 91, *92*; passerines, 85–6; waders, 87, *97*
Fieldnotes, recording of, 74, 113–4, 120–1
Finches, 69
Flight, methods of, 26–7, *27*, 90, *102*, *103*
Food chains, 14–16, *14*
Fowling, *133*, *138*, 139, *140*
Fulmar, 16, 26, 37–8, 51–2, *90*, 103–4, *115*, 124, *138*, 139,

140: defence mechanism of, 31, *31*

Gannet, *29*, 30, 32, 37, **52**, **55**, *55*, *72*, 105, *106*, 109, *109*, 124, *125*, *128*, 138, 139
Geese, 38, **56–57**: Barnacle, 57, 107–8; Brent, 29, *30*, 57, *57*, 88, 91, 122–3
Godwits, *28*: Bar-tailed, 60, 87, 113; Black-tailed, *30*, 60
Goldeneye, *33*, 57, 92, 112: Barrow's, 58
Goosander, 29, 57
Grebes, 26, 28, 29, 37, **50–1**: Black-necked, 51; Great Crested, 50, *50*, 51; Little, 50, 51, 113; Red-necked, 51; Slavonian, 51
Greenshank, 61
Guillemots, 13, 37, 42, 67, *67*, *72*, 99–101, *100*, 124, *143*, 147; Black, 42, 68, 79–80, 99–100, 146, 149; Brünnich's, 67
Gular fluttering, 32
Gulls, 19, *27*, 27, 28, 37–8, **64–6**: culling of, 150–1, increase in populations of, 45: on cliffs and islands, 99, 101–3, 105, 107; on mudflats, 86, 91; on saltmarsh, 92, 94–5; in sand dunes, 80–3; on sandy beaches, 75–6, *76*; on shingle beaches, 95–6; on rocky shores, 96–9; at sea, 108–10; on urban waterfronts, 110–11: Audouin's, 66; Black-headed, *22*, 27, 33, 65, *92*, 94–5, *111*, 150; Common, 45, 65; Glaucous, 65, *76*; Great Black-backed, *54*, 65, 83, 105–7, *107*, *111*, 138, 140; Herring, *54*, 64, 64, 65, 76, 81–3, *110*, 140, 141, *141*, 150–1; Iceland, 65, *76*; Lesser Black-backed, 45, 65, *76*, *82*, 138, 140, 141; Little, 76, 146; Mediterranean, 66; Sabine's, 66; Slender-billed, 66

Habitats, variety and function of coastal, 6–7, 11, *12*: natural succession of, 12–13, *19*; *see*

also individual habitats
Harriers, 19: Hen, 86; Marsh, 59, 86; Montagu's, 59
Havergate Island, *118*, 119, 149
Hawks, **58–9**
Heron, Grey, 27, **56**, *56*
Hides, 74, 114, 117, *119*

Ice Ages, effect on coastal habitats of, 7–11, *8*
Injured birds, care of, 127–9
Invertebrates, function in food chain of, *14*, 15–16, *15*
Irish Wildbird Conservancy, 122, 149, 154

Jackdaw, 69, 86, 91

Kestrel, 19, 58, *58*, 86
Kittiwake, 37, 38, 45, 65, 66, *71*, *100*, 102–3, 111, 124, *126*, 131, 138, 139
Kleptoparasitism, 38, 64, *85*
Knot, 7, 40, 46, 61

Lapwing, 20, 60, 81, 87
Larks, 69: Shore Lark, 69, *69*; Skylark, 69, 85
Linnaeus, 48
Linnet, 69
Long-shore drift, *17*, 22, 95
Loons, *see* Divers

Machair, 19–20
Mallard, *57*, 58, 81, 88, 94
Merganser, Red-breasted, 29, *30*, 57, 107
Merlin, 59
Migration, 13, 25, 33–4, 38–40, *39*; at sea, 108, *108*; study of, *125*, 129–36
Minsmere, *118*, 119, 149
Moult, *9*, 13, 33–4, *34*, 37
Mudflats, 6, 11, *12*, 20–1, *21*: birds on, 86–8, 91–2, *148*
Murres, *see* Guillemots

Nature Conservancy Council, 117, 129, 154

Nesting: competition for sites, 100; disturbance of, *53*, 79, *150*; requirements for, 17, 25
Nets: cannon, 131–2, *132*; fleyg, 133, *133*; mist, 131, *144*

Ocean currents, 13, *13*, 24, *24*, 99
Oiled birds, care of, 127–9, *128*; *see also* Pollution
Operation Seafarer, 124, 138
Owl, Short-eared, 19, 59, 86
Oystercatcher, 7, *28*, *30*, *35*, *36*, 38, 59, *76*, 77–8, *77*, 87–8, *95*, 96–7

Papa Westray, *118*, 148
Passerines, **69**
Peewit, 60, *see also* Lapwing
Pellets, as aid to identification, 46, 87, 107
Peregrine, 58–9, 107, 137, 146
Pesticides, *see* Pollution
Petrels, 26–7, 28, 31, **51–2**, 99: diving, 26; storm, 37, 51–2, 124; Leach's, 52, 105; Storm, 29, 52, 105, *130*, 138, *144*
Phalaropes, 28, 29, 37, 59, **63**, 98: Grey, 63, 120; Red-necked, 63, *63*
Photography, 114–7
Phytoplankton, 16
Pigeons, **68–9**
Pintail, 58, 80, 88, 122
Pipits, 69: Meadow, 69, 85; Rock, 69, 96
Plovers, 38: Golden, 60, 137; Green, 60, *see also* Lapwing; Grey, 33–4, 60; Kentish, 61; Little Ringed, 63; Ringed, 13, *28*, 61, 77–8, *96*
Pochard, 112
Pollution: oil, 37, 44, 121, *128*, 145–7; pesticide residues, 59, 145–6; toxic chemicals, 145, 148
Population dynamics, 43–5, *44*, 136, 145
Populations, estimation of seabird, 137–8; variations in, 139–142, 145–7
Predation, 25, 31, *31*, 40–1, *41*, 79, 105, 107, *107*, 148–9

Proventricular oil, 31, *31*
Puffin, 26, *30*, 42, 67, 68, *73*, 99–102, *101*, *102*, 124, *126*, 131, 139, 142–5, 147

Raven, 69, 107
Razorbill, *27*, 37, 42, 49, 68, 99–102, *103*, *116*, 124, 138, 147, 149
Reclamation, 11–12, *12*, 147, *148*
Redshank, 22, *28*, 35, 60–1, 93–4, *93*: Dusky, 47; Spotted, 47, 61, 63
Reeve, 61, *see also* Ruff
Reserves, 75, 117–9, *119*, 147, 149: map of, *118*
Ringing, 129–36, *130*, 134, *144*: map of main sites, *135*
Rock Dove, 58, 68–9, *68*, 107
Rocky shores, 6, 11, 12, *12*, 23–4, *23*: birds of, 96–9
Royal Society for the Prevention of Cruelty to Animals, 127, 129, 154
Royal Society for the Protection of Birds, 78, 117, 122, 123, 129, 139, 149, 154
Ruff, 59, 61, 93, *98*

Safety precautions in bird-watching, 75
Salt gland, use of, 30
Saltmarsh, 6, 11, 12, *12*, 21–2, 22, *148*: birds on, 92–5
Sand dunes, 6, 18–20, *19*, *148*: birds of, 80–6
Sanderling, *30*, 34, *35*, *39*, 40, 49, 63
Sandpipers: Black-bellied, 47; Broad-billed, 63; Common, *10*, 62; Curlew, 62–3; Green, 62, 93; Pectoral, 63; Purple, 23, 62, 97–8; Wood, 62, 93
Scaup, 57, 92, 111, 122
Scoter: Common, 57, 120, 147; Velvet, 57, 107, 147
Seabird Group, 121, 123, 124, 127, 154
Seaducks, 57, 120, 147
Sea, open, 6, 24; birds of, 108–10
Seawatching, 108–10, 119–22
Shag, *28*, 32, 55, 80, *89*, 105,

131, 138, 145, 146
Shearwaters, 26, 27, *27*, 29, 37, 51–2, 109: Great, 51–2, *108*; Manx, *27*, 39, *51*, 52, 103–5, *104*, *107*, 124; Sooty, 51–2
Shelduck, 20, 34, 37, 58, 60, 80–1, *81*, *94*
Shingle spit, *see* Beach
Shoveler, 29, *30*, 58, 88
Skuas, 38, **63–4**, 99, 109–10: Arctic, *63*, 64, *85*; Great, *41*, 64, 138; Long-tailed, 64; Pomarine, 64
Slimbridge, *118*, 119
Snipe, *10*, 63, 93
Starling, 69, 85–6
Stilt, Black-winged, 63
Stints, 87, 93: Little, 62; Temminck's, 62
St Kilda, *118*, *135*, *138*, 139–45
Surveys, 122–7; Beached Bird, 123
Swans, 37, **56**: Bewick's, 56; Mute, 56, *56*; Whooper, 56, 80, 81

Teal, 22, 29, *30*, 58
Telescopes, use of, 73–4, 109
Terns, 27, *27*, 28, 37–8, **66–7**, 78–9, 109, 150–1: in sand dunes, 80–1, 83–5; in urban areas, 12, *112*: Arctic, *27*, 39, 66, 83–4, *84*, 148; Black, 67; Caspian, 67; Common, 12, 66, *78*, 83–4, *85*; Fairy, 47; Gull-billed, 67; Little, 12, *53*, 67, 79, 95–6; Roseate, 22, 66–7, *66*, 83–4, 138, 142; Sandwich, 66, 83–4, *83*, 138, 141–2, 150; White, 47
Thornham, 78, *118*
Traps: heligoland, 132–3, *132*; wader, 133
Tubenoses, 51
Turnstone, *35*, 39–40, 49, 61, 62, 97–8, *97*
Twite, 69
Tystie, *see* Black Guillemot

Urban waterfronts, 6, 11–12, *12*: birds of, 110–12

Waddenzee, 34, 46, 57, 147
Waders, 28, *28*, 29, 32–3, 37, 40, **59–63**, 132: on mudflats, 86–8, *86*; on rocky shores, 96–9; on saltmarsh, 92–4; on sandy beaches, 75–8; at sea, 108–9; on shingle beaches, 95; on urban waterfronts, 110–12
Wash, The, 34, 39, 40, *118*, 122, 137
Waterproofing, of feathers, 32, *32*, 127–8
Wetlands Enquiry, 122
Whimbrel, 60
Wigeon, 38, 58
Wildfowl, 27, **56–8**; on cliffs and islands, 99, 107–8; on mudflats, 86, 88, 91–2; in sand dunes, 80–1; at sea, 108–9
Wildfowl Trust, 119, 122, 154
Wings, functions and adaptations of, 26–7, *27*, *102*, *103*
Woodpigeon, 69

Zooplankton, 16, *16*